Food for All Seasons

Savory Recipes from the Pacific Northwest

by David Pisegna

Photographs by Dick Busher

Landscape Photographs by Pat O'Hara

Chronicle Books   San Francisco

For my mother

and father

Design and composition by Wilsted & Taylor
Food styling by David Pisegna

Printed in Japan

LIBRARY OF CONGRESS CATALOGING-IN-PUBLICATION DATA
Pisegna, David.
Food for all seasons : savory recipes from the
Pacific Northwest / by David Pisegna : photographs by
Dick Busher and Pat O'Hara.
p.   cm.
Includes index.
ISBN 0-87701-733-6
1. Cookery, American—Pacific Northwest style.   I. Title.
TX715.2.P32P57   1990
641.59795—dc20   90-45883
                                                    CIP

Distributed in Canada by
Raincoast Books
112 East Third Avenue
Vancouver, B.C. V5T 1C8

10 9 8 7 6 5 4 3 2 1

Chronicle Books
275 Fifth Street
San Francisco, California 94103

CONTENTS

ACKNOWLEDGMENTS

The task of writing this book has been a joy because of the people I have had the privilege to know and of the foods, expertise and effort they have given.

I gratefully acknowledge the following people: my wife, Maureen, whose love and ability went into each of these recipes and photographs. From her hands came the wonderful cookie, preserve and muffin recipes and the polish to every word herein. Without her undying faith and understanding this book—and this man—would never have been. And Dick Busher and Pat O'Hara, who showed me the wonder of photography and gave me a greater understanding of food presentation, the landscape, and their ultimate union. Many thanks to the Ericksen family and all the people at University Seafood for the seafood presented in these photographs and for their support and good humor. Terry Bagley and all the people at Charlie's Produce for the beautiful vegetables and fruits, along with Steve Evans and all the growers and producers of Pike Place Market in Seattle. Austin Ross, Don Olson, Dr. Richard Lindeman, Jerry Rogers, Marion Watanabe, Diane Thomas, Ann Gamon, Margaret O'Leary and all the men and women of Virginia Mason Medical Center whose commitment to good food and good health has given a deeper meaning to my work. Julia Child, Graham Kerr and the American Institute of Wine and Food, a guiding light for good cooking and good living. Peggy Elliott, Peter Smith and Jim Woodrow, who were involved in the creation of these dishes and prepared them diligently and faithfully, often under difficult circumstances. Saleh Joudah of Saleh al Lago for his integrity through the most difficult stages of this project. Nion McEvoy, who believed enough in this book to put up with me, which speaks more of his patience and good appetite than of my ability. Bernice Robison, Mary Frank, Veronica Hall and Cynthia Shaw, who made order out of chaos, along with Annie Barrows, Carolyn Miller and Karen Pike of Chronicle Books. Harold Pfeiffer for his able assistance with the photography, along with Ron McLean and Mark Nishimura. Special thanks to the following artisans who created the serving ware these dishes are presented on: Pat Royce, Mud Bay Pottery, Ed Robinson, Stephen Fabrico, Susan Lochner, Savoy Studios, Tina Richardson, Dennis Meiners, Hiroski Ogawa, Sam Scott, Ken Booth, Glenn Burris, Hank Murrow, Pacifica Glass, Ernest Helsenberg, Dan Doak, Patrick Horsley, Ken Stevens, Joanne Fox, Shoshama Israel, and Larry Halvorsen. The Abbey, Jaeger, Stephens, Fredericks and Fisher-Green families, and Sister Dolores Crosby for all their support through the ups and downs. The Sweeney family for their unflappable good cheer through thick and thin.

To place my name on these pages seems unfair, for they never would have been possible without the vast array of people whose love of the Pacific Northwest and its wonderful food continues every day. It is my wish that I have represented them and the Northwest as well as they deserve.

INTRODUCTION

Good cooking involves far more than the act of measuring, or the movement of hand to knife, or of meat to skillet. The deceivingly simple act of turning raw foodstuffs into nourishment and pleasure unites us with the earth, the seas, and the constancy of the seasons. To cook with exuberance, awareness, and joyousness, we must open our hearts to the world of dew-covered gardens, alpine light, fiery sunsets, languid bays, and fragrant forests. For each day of each season changes our lives, beginning with spring's first cherries, the nectar of sweet scallops and oysters, tart berries, fragrant apples and pears, rich and aromatic mushrooms. That perfect luscious tomato, peach, or strawberry is summer in the hand. Autumn's tawny venison, duck, and pheasant, and winter's aromas of the smoker, simmering stews, and rich chowders—each taste, each smell, is a revelation.

A map, a musical score, a recipe, each offers a path, a rhythm inviting us to join in, to discover and partake of moments transcending the lines, notes and measurements on the page. There is no fulfillment of sight, sound, or taste without the enjoyment of those involved in its creation.

A recipe combines the guides and intricacies of orchestration so that reader and cook become both the leader and the guide, free to explore the boundaries of the score and to be carried beyond its limits. These recipes offer the same welcoming hand with the hope you will bring your own love of cooking to their preparation, create them and make them your own. Read the recipes before beginning: you will know the direction and can more easily blend the steps with your schedule and your own touches. They are structured to allow one to prepare them in stages for a quick assembly to fit into busy family life, and also to involve the cook, family and friends, so that the journey is as much fun as the destination.

If there is a golden rule it is to *enjoy* each step: the procurement, cooking and sharing with others. Our greatest wish is that in preparing these foods you come to a deeper appreciation of the art of cooking and the land in which you live. Bring care and sensibility to the kitchen and you will be rewarded a thousandfold each time you cook.

There can be few places more wonderful to cook in than the Pacific Northwest. Beaches of clams, oysters, and mussels make a clam shovel and bucket a kitchen necessity, and a crab pot and fishing pole are as important as a skillet. Northwest cooking was born from glistening seafood and the fruits of its mountains and fields, and we take part in the beauty of this land with every morsel. It is the special province of the cook to make sunsets glow on the plate, to create with each dish a world of color, taste, and texture that preserves the connection between land and table. The superb foods of this region keep us aware that heaven is as close as the path we tread, the fish we fillet, the nuts we grind, the stews and soups we simmer.

We can understand cooking first through history. American cooking still may be in its youth, but it is the product of many different cultures. The famed melting pot was really a "donation stew," created by pioneers in the western wilderness, to which everyone brought what he or she could, resulting in a dish much more than the sum of its parts. The Native American gathering berries for winter, dipping nets in churning rivers full of salmon, drying strips of fish over alder fires; the pioneer woman with her recipes for mincemeat, sourdough, and biscuits passed down for hundreds of years from mother to mother; the boy learning to hunt and fish to provide food for his family; the barn raisings, socials, campfires and canneries, potlatches, and celebrations of people of every background and heritage—all are part of the history of this abundant land.

On May 1, 1792, when Captain Vancouver anchored in the Strait of San Juan de Fuca, the numerous Native American tribes of what are now Oregon, Washington, and British Columbia had a fully developed system of harvesting and preserving a wide variety of native foods. Roots, nuts, berries, and salmon were the staples and had been in the centuries since human beings first crossed the ice bridge over the Bering Sea. The traditional harvesting and cooking techniques of the Native Americans, and their worship of the natural world as sacred, are an enduring heritage in the culture of the Pacific Northwest.

Settlers came, following Lewis and Clark along the Oregon Trail in the early 1840s. The rich, fertile valleys of the Oregon Territory were settled first. Gradually settlers headed north, and by 1880 the group of peoples that "made do or did without" included Russians, Chinese, Japanese, Vietnamese, Thai, Koreans, Spaniards, Mexicans, French, Canadians, English, Croatians, and Scandinavians.

Then on July 17, 1897, forty-five miners walked off the steamship *Portland* at the Seattle docks. The *Portland* had come down from the Yukon, and the men aboard carried over a ton of gold among them. The Alaskan Gold Rush had begun. Hordes of prospectors, merchants, dreamers, and fortune-seekers came through Seattle on their way to Alaska. The city grew up overnight, filled with men "looking for a connection."

Soon settlers developed prospering farms in the benevolent climate, and, in 1907, the Pike Place Market was founded in Seattle. Now quantities of foodstuffs were funneled through the city—salmon, oysters, halibut, pickled and salted cod—and shipped to points all over the world. It was an era of great growth but also one of wanton waste. The beds of the oysters that graced tables in San Francisco and New York were ravaged by over-harvesting and by the damaging effects of logging on the watershed. The land began to show the first scars of development and prosperity.

When gold fever died, the Northwest was a different world, and new additions to its cooking reflected the changes, from blackberry pie to German nut loaves to dim sum. The wagon trains left a legacy of brown bread, rice pudding, soda bread, pandowdy, sauerbrauten, and hasenpfeffer. The grain farms and logging camps offered their contributions of rib-sticking stews and sourdough. It was a time of a handful of this and a pinch of that, and soon each settlement had its special dishes.

Blending with the pioneer spirit of self-reliance came wealth, civility, and culture for those who had been the most successful in the new land. In 1913, the *Oregon Women's Exchange Cookbook*, filled with sophisticated recipes, was published by the women of Portland. Suddenly, along with johnnycakes and pemmican, the Northwest was the home of cream of chestnut and artichoke soup, crab gumbo, bouillabaisse, halibut niçoise, shad roe, sweetbreads, chicken in sauterne jelly, broiled squabs on toast, curries, halibut cheek salad, charlottes, meringues, and apple snow (a concoction of pureed spiced apples and frothy egg whites reminiscent of the "Indian ice cream" made from soapberries). Other dishes included fish and oyster pies, beef à la mode, and steamed huckleberry pudding.

In a brief period of time, Northwest cooking had blossomed from subsistence meals over a campfire to elegant repasts served on silver and china. And still more settlers came, from the fur traders of the Hudson Bay Company to the workers in the burgeoning canneries, from the dairy, fish, and produce merchants, to the farmers of the wheat lands. Towns such as Spokane, Wenatchee, Salem, and Astoria grew almost overnight.

This same spirit is the guiding light of Northwest cooking today. The influence of the Pacific Rim and the influx of a new breed of settlers seeking the good life are creating growth and change in the Northwest. It is now more important than ever to preserve the land and waters that provide us with so many wonderful foods. Our fishing grounds are already in danger of depletion, and even now our forests are being ravaged. The steps we take today will shape not just the cuisine of the Northwest, but its ecological future, the delicate balance between humans and nature.

The foods of the Northwest have a rich and exciting past. Born of this beautiful land, they promise to become the basis of one of our country's most interesting and authentic regional cuisines. The Pacific Northwest is a special place, like no other on earth. The bright sky above the splendor of our oceans and mountains is our only limit, the riches below are our sustenance.

A NOTE ON INGREDIENTS

Wholesome cooking and good eating go hand in hand. These recipes, while not intended to be "diet cooking," are created both for great taste and good health. Sauces are prepared using a moderate quantity of fats and are intended to be used in small quantities, 1 tablespoon to 1 ounce per serving. While cream is used widely, it is used in small quantities in soups and sauces. If butterfat is a concern, simply substitute milk, yogurt, or spoon cheese (see page 164) for cream. Butter is specified in many recipes and may be replaced with margarine. Sugar is also used in moderation, but with many dishes it is an integral component. Non-nutritive sweeteners such as Sweet and Low and Suscatel can be used in many baked goods following manufacturers' equivalent measurements. More importantly, for many of the desserts, a little piece goes a long way.

Balance your cooking and your diet with complex carbohydrates and fiber, monitor your intake of fats—a sensible amount can be enjoyable, too. For, above all, the enjoyment of good cooking is the enjoyment of good living. We carry the responsibility to take care of ourselves and our families, and good cooking that stresses well-prepared fresh ingredients is the best possible way to do so. The additives, preservatives, and chemicals of processed foods burden us with harming ourselves and the natural world, but this is a vicious cycle that we have the power to change.

With good sense, the art of cooking—heart, hand, body, and mind—can transform us. To prepare a dish from garden or market to table nourishes us completely, again and again, forever.

SPRING

SPRING

Blustery squalls, wisps of fir smoke, bright swelling waters, and mountain fog—this is spring in the Pacific Northwest.

The warming, rich earth offers greater prizes every day: another handful of peas, sweet onions, tender lettuce, fragrant thyme. Soon there will be cherries from Yakima; their blossoms have already opened in the breaking grayness, and as the days grow longer, the winds grow calmer and warmer. The bounty of the sea returns: halibut, oysters, mussels, cod, sturgeon, Dungeness crab, and, the highlight of the season, spring chinook from the Columbia River to Alaska.

With every new sprout, the world of flavor opens. Hillsides explode in bright greenness, and clouds unfold soft, sweet breezes, filling kitchens from Wenatchee to Westport, Hood River to Depot Bay, with the fragrance of moist earth and blossom fragrance, crab pots and tidepools.

The dishes in this chapter are born of the brightness and clarity of this wonderful season. Oysters, scallops, sea urchins, halibut cheeks, trout and steelhead, and sturgeon are at their peak in early spring, along with succulent lamb, morels, asparagus, peas, and salad greens. The first strawberries arrive to be used for shortcakes, pies, jams, and eating out of hand.

Combining the flavors of the cuisines of the Pacific Rim with traditional American dishes gives a new dimension to the treasures of spring. The Asian techniques of slow steaming and flash cooking add a distinctive touch to the day's market finds and invite us to explore the ever-growing world of cooking in the Northwest.

The best kind of cooking highlights the main ingredient, using seasonings and flavors that complement rather than overshadow or muddle its taste. Restraint and control, both in conception and technique, are imperative. We learn this lesson again most vividly in spring when we hold the first foods of the year in our hands. To do much more than to season and cook these wonders as simply as possible is unnecessary. Let these foods show you the way. You will not be disappointed.

There are no secrets to this cooking; each dish is a simple, shared discovery of spring in the Pacific Northwest.

Spring Recipes

Baked Oysters with Shiitake Tapenade and Zucchini

Steamed Lamb Dumplings with Mustard Greens, Coriander, and Sage

Chilled Olympia Oysters and Smoked Sablefish with Nappa Cabbage and Lovage Salad

Spring Soup with Sugar Snap Peas

Asparagus Consommé

Sea Urchin Bisque

Morels with Asparagus and Gooseberries

Risotto with Pink Scallops, Asparagus, and Lemon Balm

Oysters and Scallops with Sea Beans and Tarragon

Spring Salmon with New Potatoes and Chervil

Grilled Steelhead with Radishes and Pennyroyal

Grilled Sturgeon and Oysters with Basil and Mango Sauces

Sautéed Rainbow Trout with Swiss Chard and Chive Blossom Vinegar

Lamb Medallions with Morels and Anise Hyssop

Roast Lamb Loin with Wild Greens and Red Currants

Hot Cherry Tarts with Rose Geranium

Strawberry-Rhubarb Cookies

Steamed Lamb Dumplings with Mustard Greens, Coriander, and Sage

Baked Oysters
with Shiitake Tapenade and Zucchini

Serves 4

Definitely not a "gild-the-lily" preparation for oysters in the shell. This heady, aromatic appetizer can also be served uncooked. Be sure to watch the cooking time closely—and it's a good idea to prepare more oysters than usual, as they disappear quickly.

24 oysters in the shell
3 garlic cloves
4 ounces fresh shiitakes, or ¼ cup dried shiitakes
2 tablespoons extra-virgin olive oil
2 tablespoons Marsala
2 to 3 pitted Calamata or any good-quality olives
1 tablespoon minced fresh basil
1 tablespoon minced fresh oregano
1 teaspoon minced fresh parsley
1 medium zucchini, shredded (about 1½ cups shredded)
Salt and pepper to taste
Extra-virgin olive oil for brushing
2 tablespoons fine bread crumbs

Preheat the oven to 400°. Wash the oysters and shuck them, reserving all of the liquor and the cupped half shells. Dry each cupped shell and rub it well with 1 of the garlic cloves. Mince the remaining garlic cloves and reserve.

Wash the shiitakes well and cut in ½-inch strips. If using dried mushrooms, cover with cold water for 15 minutes until softened, squeeze dry, and cut into ½-inch strips. Heat the olive oil in a heavy, medium skillet and add the shiitakes. Sauté, tossing well, for 1 minute. Add the Marsala and olives and sauté for 1 minute; remove from the heat.

Place the shiitake mixture in a blender or a food processor and blend until the mixture is coarsely pureed. Add the minced herbs and blend. Remove the tapenade from the blender or food processor and set aside at room temperature.

Place the oyster shells in a bed of rock salt in a heavy baking pan. Divide the tapenade and the shredded zucchini equally among the shells, seasoning with salt, pepper, and the reserved minced garlic. Top each with an oyster. Brush with extra-virgin olive oil and spread with a light layer of tapenade. Sprinkle with the bread crumbs. Bake in the preheated oven for 4 to 5 minutes, or until the oyster gills begin to curl. Brush again with olive oil and serve immediately.

Steamed Lamb Dumplings
with Mustard Greens, Coriander, and Sage

Makes 16 dumplings, or 4 servings

The perfect appetizer: it leaves you wanting to make a whole meal of these delicious dumplings, which is not a bad idea at all. *Myoga*, a slightly lemony and mildly spicy ginger shoot, adds a delightful touch. These dumplings are also excellent served chilled.

Baked Oysters with Shiitake Tapenade and Zucchini

DUMPLINGS

12 ounces lamb (from shoulder or leg), cubed
1 ounce (¼ cup) lamb fat
1 teaspoon minced fresh sage
1 teaspoon minced fresh parsley
1 teaspoon minced fresh chives
1 teaspoon minced fresh myoga (available in Asian
  markets), optional; or ½ teaspoon minced fresh lemon
  grass or fresh ginger
2 teaspoons soy sauce or tamari
¼ teaspoon ground coriander
⅛ teaspoon minced fresh ginger
Salt and fresh-ground black pepper to taste (if not using
  ginger as a replacement for myoga)
1 package wonton wrappers (available in Asian markets)

STEAMING LIQUID

1 cup sake or dry white wine
1 teaspoon coriander seed, crushed
1 star anise
2 tablespoons soy sauce or tamari
1 teaspoon dried orange peel
1 tablespoon minced myoga (available in Asian markets),
  optional; or 1½ teaspoons minced fresh lemon grass or
  ginger

16 small fresh sage leaves
1 bunch mustard greens
Salt and pepper to taste
Asian (toasted) sesame oil to taste
Rice vinegar to taste

To make the dumplings   In a large glass or ceramic bowl, toss the lamb and lamb fat with the herbs, soy sauce, and spices. Season lightly with salt and pepper. Refrigerate for 4 hours, stirring occasionally. Remove to a cutting surface and, with a sharp knife, chop the meat fine, but not to a paste. Brush each wonton wrapper lightly with water. Roll 1 tablespoon of the lamb mixture into a ball and place in the center of each wrapper, gath-

ering the edges to the center in a star shape; seal with your fingers. Cover the wontons with a cloth until all are filled.

To make the steaming liquid   Place the sake, coriander, anise, soy sauce, orange peel, and *myoga* in a wok. Cover and simmer for 5 minutes. Place the dumplings in a bamboo steamer insert or in a stainless steel steamer basket. Place a sage leaf on each dumpling, set the insert or basket in the wok (on a trivet, if necessary), and cover. Steam for 5 to 8 minutes.

Meanwhile, wash the mustard greens and remove the stems. Tear the greens into even pieces and place in a small bowl. Season with salt and pepper. Sprinkle lightly with the oil and vinegar and toss. Arrange on 4 plates and place the dumplings around. Serve immediately, with the steaming liquid on the side as a dipping sauce.

Chilled Olympia Oysters
and Smoked Sablefish
with Nappa Cabbage
and Lovage Salad

Serves 4

The tiny Olympia oyster, once near devastation from overharvesting and pollution, has been saved by conscientious aquaculture. One of the hallmarks of Northwest cuisine, these oysters are best served on the half shell, unadorned. Sablefish or black cod, a buttery fish that is excellent smoked, makes this dish a fish-lover's dream. You can cure and smoke your own fish very easily, as the recipe explains, or buy commercially smoked fish.

8 ounces smoked or fresh sablefish, cod, trout, or whitefish
*   fillet*
1½ to 2 cups finely shredded Nappa cabbage
2 tablespoons lovage, celery, or curly endive leaves
2 to 3 tablespoons Basic Vinaigrette, page 165
1½ teaspoons minced fresh parsley
1 teaspoon minced fresh chives
Juice of ½ lemon
Salt and fresh-ground black pepper to taste
Lovage leaves for garnish
24 to 32 Olympia oysters in the shell

To smoke your own sablefish: Cure the fresh sablefish as described on page 152. Refrigerate the fish uncovered for at least 2 hours, or overnight. Remove the cured sablefish from the refrigerator and, if possible, place a household fan so that it will blow air over the fillet for 1 hour to glaze the surface.

Prepare the smoker and smoke the sablefish as directed on page 152. Cool to room temperature and refrigerate until well chilled, about 2 hours. The recipe can be prepared a day in advance to this point.

Place the Nappa cabbage in a glass or ceramic bowl. Tear the lovage into small bite-sized pieces and toss lightly with the cabbage. Add the vinaigrette, herbs, lemon juice, and salt and pepper. Toss again and refrigerate until well chilled, about 1 hour. At the same time, place 4 serving plates in the freezer, along with 4 shallow bowls about 3 inches in diameter.

Slice the smoked sablefish into 8 equal slices and set aside. Crack enough ice in a kitchen towel or plastic bag to fill the small bowls. Place the bowls of ice on the plates, allowing enough room to arrange the salad and sablefish attractively on the plates. Garnish with the lovage leaves.

Shuck the oysters, reserving all of the liquor and the cupped half shells. Place the oysters in the half shells and top with reserved liquor. Arrange the shells on the bowls of ice and serve immediately.

Spring Soup with Sugar Snap Peas

Serves 4

This delicious soup is the color of emeralds, and is full of the taste of spring. The richness of the vegetable broth is heightened by the fresh sweetness of pureed peas, whisked into the soup at the last minute.

1 medium onion
1 medium carrot
1 celery stalk
1 small leek
1 medium turnip
4 shallots
1 tablespoon peanut oil
2 thyme sprigs
2 tarragon sprigs
2 garlic cloves, crushed
4 cups (1 quart) Chicken Stock, page 158, or canned chicken broth

GARNISH
3 cups sugar snap peas in the pod, or 3 cups shelled peas
12 asparagus stalks
½ cup heavy cream
1 teaspoon cornstarch dissolved in 1 teaspoon water

¼ cup julienne-cut carrot
¼ cup julienne-cut leek (white part only)
2 tablespoons julienne-cut beet
¼ cup julienne-cut yellow squash
4 squash blossoms (optional)

Mince the onion, carrot, celery, leek, turnip, and shallots. Heat the peanut oil in a heavy saucepan or skillet and add the vegetables, herbs, and garlic; cover and cook over low heat without browning for 20 minutes. Remove any fat from the chicken stock and add the stock to the pan. Bring to a boil. Reduce to a simmer and cook for 20 minutes. Strain the liquid through a fine sieve, pressing all the liquid out of the vegetables. Set aside at room temperature.

To prepare the garnish, trim the pods if using whole peas. Blanch the peas for 10 seconds in boiling salted water, drain, and immerse immediately in ice water. Drain and chop coarse. Trim the asparagus and cut it into 1-inch lengths.

Place 1 cup of the peas and a little of the cooled soup in a blender or food processor and puree until very smooth; repeat with the remaining peas, in 1-cup batches. Press the contents of the blender through a fine sieve. Reheat the stock until almost boiling and add the cream. Whisk in the cornstarch mixture and bring to a simmer and vigorously whip in the pea puree. Divide the julienne-cut garnishes among 4 heated wide-rim soup bowls and pour the soup over. Garnish with the squash blossoms, if desired. Serve immediately.

Spring Soup with Sugar Snap Peas

Asparagus Consommé

Serves 6

This is the perfect spring tonic and a great way to use up extra asparagus stalks. The addition of julienne-cut chicken, pheasant, or ham makes a heartier soup or lunch main course. Poached oysters, scallops, or other seafood or shellfish are also delicious. Be sure to save any leftover consommé, as it makes a delicious stock for steaming vegetables or seafood.

1 to 1½ pounds asparagus
1½ to 2 quarts cold Chicken Stock, page 158, or canned
  chicken broth
½ small onion
1 celery stalk
½ carrot
3 shallots
2 bay leaves
3 parsley sprigs
2 tarragon sprigs
2 thyme sprigs
½ teaspoon black peppercorns, crushed
4 to 6 egg whites
3 cloves
Pinch each ground mace, ginger, cinnamon, and allspice

GARNISH
6 quail eggs
Reserved asparagus tips
¼ to ½ cup julienne-cut cooked chicken, ham, pheasant,
  quail, or duck (optional)
Fresh thyme, tarragon, chervil, or parsley sprigs for garnish

Remove the stems of the asparagus 1½ inches from the tips, reserving the tips. Chop the stems, and puree them in a blender or food processor with ½ cup of the chicken stock. Remove the asparagus from the blender or food processor. Add the onion, celery, carrot, shallots, bay leaves, and herbs to the machine and chop fine. Combine with the asparagus stems. Add the egg whites and the dried spices. The mixture should have the consistency of wet sand. Add an additional ½ to 1 cup chicken stock if necessary.

Remove any fat from the remaining chicken stock and combine the stock with the asparagus mixture in a heavy, 6-quart saucepan, blending well. Over low heat, stirring occasionally to prevent the mixture from sticking, bring the consommé to a simmer. As it approaches a simmer, a "raft" (a coagulation of the egg whites, vegetables, and spices) will begin to form. When it has fully solidified, stop stirring the consommé. Adjust the heat so the consommé barely bubbles through the raft in 1 or 2 places. Continue to simmer for 25 minutes.

Remove the consommé from the heat and allow to sit undisturbed for 10 minutes. Carefully remove the raft from the surface with a slotted spoon and discard. Once most of the raft is removed, strain the consommé through a fine sieve lined with a dampened piece of double-layered cheesecloth. The consommé should be crystal clear, with no trace of the clarification raft.

Cook the quail eggs in boiling water to cover for 2 to 3 minutes. Drain and cool, peel, and cut them in half. Transfer the consommé to a saucepan and bring to a simmer; do not boil. To make the garnish, place 6 to 8 asparagus tips per person (less if using poultry or meat garnishes) in a strainer and blanch in the simmering consommé for 3 minutes, or until bright green.

Divide the asparagus tips, quail eggs, and julienne-cut poultry or meat, if desired, among 4 hot wide-rim soup bowls. Bring the consommé barely to a boil, adjust the seasoning to taste, and ladle it into the bowls. Garnish with the herbs and serve immediately.

Sea Urchin Bisque

Serves 4

Sea urchins are the quintessential taste of the sea. Their flavor is delicate, however, and they must be handled with the utmost care.

12 small sea urchins, or 2 ounces sea urchin roe
Double recipe Vin Blanc Sauce, page 162
½ to ¾ cup heavy cream
¾ to 1 cup Fish Stock, page 157, or bottled clam juice
1 lime
Salt and pepper to taste
4 dill, fennel, or tarragon sprigs

If not using the sea urchins immediately after purchase, refrigerate them in sea water or on ice for maximum of 24 hours.

Prepare the Vin Blanc Sauce. Wash the sea urchins well and, holding each one on its side, slice off the top with a sharp knife, allowing the water to drain out. Immediately check the sea urchin. It should smell freshly of the sea and have a firm, well-formed inner body with orange-colored roe. Scoop out the roe, discarding the remaining urchin. Continue until all of the urchins are cleaned. Reserve 4 of the most attractive roe.

Puree the remaining sea urchin roe in a blender or food processor until very smooth. You should have approximately ½ cup of sea urchin puree. Reserve 1 tablespoon of the puree. Add the cream, a tablespoon at a time, to the Vin Blanc Sauce; then add the puree, a tablespoon at a time, according to taste, and puree in a blender or a food processor for 2 to 3 minutes, or until very smooth; thin with fish stock as necessary.

Slice 4 very thin slices from the lime. Squeeze the juice from the remainder of the lime and add 1 to 2 teaspoons to the bisque to taste. The bisque should have a delicate sea urchin taste with a slight hint of lime. Bring the soup to the simmer and adjust the seasoning lightly. The bisque will need little or no salt. Ladle the soup into preheated bowls, float a lime slice on each, and garnish with 1 of the reserved roe, spooning decorative swirls of the reserved urchin puree over the soup. Garnish with the dill sprigs and serve immediately.

Morels with Asparagus and Gooseberries

Serves 4

These woodland treasures have an incomparable flavor. Simply sautéed, their uses are thousandfold, and the taste they bring to any dish is ethereal. Morels freeze well packed tightly in plastic containers and covered with peanut oil, and are also delicious pickled (see page 166). Sautéed with the finest first asparagus of spring and graced with this simple sauce, they are spectacular as an appetizer or as a vegetable with meat, poultry, veal, lamb, or game.

1 pound asparagus
¾ to 1 pound morels or other wild mushrooms (oyster
*   mushrooms, chanterelles, cèpes, etc.), or 3 ounces dried*
*   mushrooms*
1 cup gooseberries, stemmed
1 teaspoon sugar
1 fresh thyme sprig, or ⅛ teaspoon minced fresh thyme
1 teaspoon peanut oil
1 shallot, minced
Salt and fresh-ground white pepper to taste
3 tablespoons Marsala or port
2 tablespoons heavy cream
2 to 3 tablespoons butter

Trim 1 inch from the bottom of the asparagus. Blanch the asparagus in boiling salted water for 3 minutes, or until bright green; drain and immerse in ice water. Drain. Place the morels in a bowl and add water to cover. Stir with your hands to remove all traces of dirt from the cavities of the morels, and drain immediately. Dry with paper towels. If using dried mushrooms, soak in cold water to cover for 15 to 20 minutes, then drain and squeeze dry.

In a small saucepan, simmer 3 tablespoons of the gooseberries with the sugar over low heat until softened. Puree in a blender or food processor. Return to low heat and reduce to a thick syrup; set aside. Remove the leaves from the thyme sprig and mince.

Heat a heavy skillet over high heat. Add the oil, shallot, and morels. Toss for 30 seconds, seasoning with salt and pepper. Add the remaining gooseberries, thyme, and asparagus and cover. Steam for 30 seconds. Remove morels to a warm plate and keep warm. Add the Marsala to skillet and reduce to a glaze. Add the cream and reduce until slightly thickened. Remove from the heat. Whisk in the butter and the gooseberry puree. Keep warm.

Divide the sauce among 4 warm plates. Place the morels in the center and arrange the asparagus and gooseberries around them. Serve immediately.

Morels with Asparagus and Gooseberries

Risotto with Pink Scallops, Asparagus, and Lemon Balm

Serves 4

A hearty, satisfying dish for the lingering chill of a Northwest spring. Pink scallops are abundant in upper Puget Sound, from the Strait of Juan de Fuca all the way to Vancouver Island. Bay scallops are an excellent substitute if pink scallops are not available, but the unique taste of "singing pinks" is well worth the effort to find them.

2 to 3 dozen pink scallops in the shell, or 8 ounces bay scallops
½ cup dry white wine
16 to 20 asparagus tips, 1½ inches to 2 inches in length
3 tablespoons olive oil
1 tablespoon minced onion
1 teaspoon minced garlic
1½ cups Italian Arborio rice or converted rice
4 to 5 cups hot Fish Stock, page 157, or bottled clam juice
¼ cup heavy cream
Salt and pepper to taste
2 tablespoons fresh lemon balm or sorrel leaves, finely shredded

Wash the pink scallops well. Pour the wine into a large skillet and bring to a simmer. Add the scallops, cover the skillet tightly, and steam until the scallops open, about 2 minutes. If using bay scallops, steam just until plumped, about 1 minute. Strain the scallop juices and reserve. Cool the scallops and remove them from the shells, trimming the green sac from the base of each scallop. Reserve a few shells for garnish. Blanch the asparagus in boiling salted water for about 3 minutes, or until bright green; immerse in ice water until cooled, then drain and set aside.

Heat the oil in a large saucepan and sauté the onion over low heat until translucent. Add the garlic and toast lightly. Add the rice and stir until well coated. Add the reserved pink scallop liquor and, stirring constantly, cook until absorbed. Add the fish stock ½ cup at a time and continue stirring and adding liquid until the rice is al dente. (If desired, this process can also be done in a preheated 375° oven. Add the stock, stir, and place the pan uncovered in the oven for 5 minutes at a time, stirring twice.)

Add the cream, stirring well, and cook until the cream is absorbed. Add the scallops and the asparagus to the hot rice. Toss until heated through. Adjust the seasoning and stir in the lemon balm. Serve immediately, garnished with the reserved shells if desired.

Oysters and Scallops
with Sea Beans and Tarragon

Serves 4

This dish is the epitome of spring in the Northwest: serene and fleeting. The dish is simple, yet each step must be precisely executed. A split-second glance away from the stove and these wonderful tastes will be lost. Sea beans, or salnicornia, grow abundantly in salt marshes, and their texture and sea-like flavor provide an interesting taste to this dish.

8 oysters in the shell
10 to 12 large sea scallops
½ bunch fresh tarragon
2 parsley sprigs
1 teaspoon minced shallot
3 teaspoons peanut oil
½ cup dry white wine
2 tablespoons heavy cream
3 tablespoons butter, softened
Salt and fresh-ground white pepper to taste
¼ teaspoon fresh lemon juice
1½ to 2 cups fresh sea beans or green beans

Rinse the oysters well and shuck them, reserving all of the liquor. Slice the scallops lengthwise into ½-inch slices. Dry the oysters and scallops and set aside on paper towels. Reserve 4 sprigs of tarragon for garnish. Chop the leaves of the remaining tarragon with the parsley and set aside.

In a skillet, sauté the shallot in 1 teaspoon of the peanut oil until translucent. Add the white wine and reduce by half; add the cream and boil to reduce until slightly thickened. Puree the reduced liquid in a blender or food processor with the chopped herbs, and add the butter in small amounts. Season lightly with salt, pepper, and lemon juice; strain and keep warm.

If using green beans, cut them into 1-inch lengths. Blanch in boiling salted water for about 8 minutes, or until crisp-tender; rinse in cold water, dry, and set aside.

Heat a heavy skillet over high heat until smoking. Add 1 teaspoon of the peanut oil and quickly place the scallops in the pan. Season with salt and white pepper and brown lightly for 10 seconds. Remove to a warm platter and keep warm. Reheat the skillet. Add the remaining 1 teaspoon peanut oil, add the oysters, and season. Sauté for 10 seconds, remove, and keep warm with the scallops. Add the sea beans or green beans to the skillet and toss lightly to heat through.

Divide the sea beans or green beans in the center of 4 heated plates and arrange the scallops and oysters around them. Add the reserved oyster liquid to the tarragon sauce and spoon the sauce around. Garnish with the reserved tarragon sprigs and serve immediately.

Oysters and Scallops with Sea Beans and Tarragon

Spring Salmon
with New Potatoes and Chervil

Serves 4

This salmon dish is one of the best examples of the rule that good cooking is the process of highlighting the taste of the main ingredient. The first run of chinook salmon from Oregon's Columbia River begins in March and April and goes all the way north to the Fraser River in Canada in June. These are some of the most delicious fish of the year. Combined with the first potatoes of the season and tender chervil, spring salmon brightens many a cloudy day and is one of the dishes most evocative of the Northwest.

Four 6-ounce salmon fillets (Columbia River, Copper River,
  Fraser River, or other good-quality salmon)
3½ to 4 cups (1½ pounds) white or red new potatoes
5 tablespoons butter, softened
1 shallot, chopped
¼ cup white wine vinegar
⅓ cup heavy cream
Salt and pepper to taste
Peanut oil for brushing
½ bunch chervil

Light a wood or charcoal fire in an open grill, or preheat the broiler. Be sure the salmon fillets are of equal thickness; remove the lower belly wall and any bones with a sharp knife. Slice the potatoes into ¼-inch slices and set aside in water.

Heat 1 teaspoon of the butter in a small saucepan and sauté the shallot until it is translucent. Add the wine vinegar and reduce until almost dry. Add the cream, boil to reduce until slightly thickened, and whip in 3 tablespoons of the butter. Strain and keep warm.

Cook the potatoes in boiling salted water until three-fourths done, about 10 minutes; drain. Season the salmon with salt and pepper and brush lightly with oil. When the fire has burned down to white-red coals, grill over the hottest part of the fire for 2 minutes. Turn the fillets and move them to the side of the fire for about 4 minutes, depending on the thickness of the fish. Or cook under the broiler, 3 to 4 inches from the element, 2 to 3 minutes per side. The salmon is done when it is just barely opaque in the center.

Meanwhile, place the potatoes in even layers in a medium-sized skillet. Season with salt and pepper and dot with the remaining butter. Cover the skillet and place over medium heat for 2 minutes, or until the potatoes are heated through and dry. Shake the pan gently to prevent sticking, being careful not to break the potatoes. Mince the chervil leaves fine, reserving 4 attractive sprigs for garnish.

Arrange the potatoes in circles on 4 preheated plates. Place each fillet on top of the potatoes. Add the minced chervil to the sauce and spoon a small amount of sauce on each plate. Garnish each plate with a chervil sprig and serve immediately.

Grilled Steelhead
with Radishes and Pennyroyal

Serves 4

The steelhead is a salmon trout that lives in both fresh and salt water. The prize gamefish in the Northwest, it has firm, light pink flesh, both delicate and robust. Pennyroyal, a pungent member of the mint family, combines with peppery, sweet icicle radishes to make a perfect setting for this superb fish.

Grilled Steelhead with Radishes and Pennyroyal

1 bunch white icicle radishes
1 bunch red radishes
5 pennyroyal, thyme, or mint sprigs
2 parsley sprigs
½ cup extra-virgin olive oil
Salt and white pepper to taste
Four 6-ounce steelhead fillets
1 tablespoon butter

Prepare a wood or charcoal fire in an open grill or preheat the broiler. Peel the white radishes, but not the red. Leave 1 inch of the tops attached if desired. Blanch the radishes in rapidly boiling salted water for approximately 1 minute. Immerse in ice water and drain; set aside.

Mince the leaves of 1 pennyroyal sprig, along with the parsley. Puree in a blender with the olive oil on medium speed for 3 minutes. The strength of pennyroyal varies, so add it in small amounts, tasting as you proceed for a light, subtle taste. Season with salt and pepper; strain through a fine sieve, pressing out all of the oil, and set aside.

When the fire has burned down to white-red coals and the grill rack is well heated, brush the fish with the herbed oil and season with salt and white pepper. Grill for 2 to 3 minutes over the hottest part of the fire, then turn and move the fish away from the center of the fire. Grill until the fish is firm to the touch, about 2 to 5 minutes, depending on the thickness of the fillets and the desired degree of doneness. If using a broiler, broil 3 to 4 inches from the element for 3 to 4 minutes per side. Meanwhile, in a medium skillet, heat the butter until foaming and add the white and red radishes. Season lightly and toss over high heat for 1 minute.

Place a steelhead fillet on each of 4 plates and arrange the radishes around the fish, garnishing each with a sprig of pennyroyal. Spoon approximately 1 tablespoon of the pennyroyal oil over each fillet and serve at once.

Grilled Sturgeon and Oysters
with Basil and Mango Sauces

Serves 4

Columbia River sturgeon is a rich, flavorful fish that combines all of the best qualities of salmon, halibut, and swordfish. It is fabulous combined with oysters and is best if grilled underdone and allowed to finish cooking on heated plates. While mangoes are not indigenous to the Northwest, they arrive in the markets from Mexico and Hawaii in spring, and their taste is too good to pass up. Baked tomatoes filled with spring vegetables go well with this dish.

12 extra-small oysters in the shell
Four 6-ounce white sturgeon fillets
2 thyme sprigs
2 tarragon sprigs
2 garlic cloves
2 tablespoons peanut oil
Salt and pepper to taste
Vin Blanc Sauce, page 162
1 ripe mango
2 tablespoons Fish Stock, page 157, or bottled clam juice
6 tablespoons butter
2 parsley sprigs
¼ cup basil leaves, plus 4 to 6 leaves for garnish

Prepare a wood or charcoal fire in an open grill, or preheat the broiler. Wash the oysters and shuck them, reserving all their liquor. Skewer 3 oysters on each of 4 bamboo or metal skewers. In a non-aluminum container, place the sturgeon, skewered oysters, herbs, garlic, and oil. Season with salt and pepper. Let sit at room temperature for 15 to 30 minutes, as desired.

Prepare the Vin Blanc Sauce; place one half of the sauce in

Grilled Sturgeon and Oysters with Basil and Mango Sauces

the refrigerator to cool to tepid for the basil sauce. Peel the mango, reserving all of the juice. Add the juice and one third of the mango to a blender or food processor. Blend on high speed until smooth and add the warm Vin Blanc Sauce and the fish stock. Blend until very smooth. Add 2 tablespoons of the butter, adjust the seasoning, and strain; place in a small saucepan and keep warm over low heat.

Add the tepid Vin Blanc Sauce to the blender or food processor with the parsley, basil, and the remaining 4 tablespoons of butter; blend until smooth. Adjust the seasoning and strain through a fine sieve. Place in a small saucepan and warm over low heat.

When the coals are white-red or the broiler is heated, remove the sturgeon and the oyster skewers from the marinade, blotting any excess oil from their surfaces. Salt and pepper both and place the sturgeon on the grill or under the broiler. If cut ½ inch thick, the sturgeon should take about 3 minutes on the first side and 1 minute on the other. When turning the sturgeon on its second side, place the oyster skewers on the grill.

Whisk the reserved oyster liquor into the basil sauce. Divide each of the 2 sauces among 4 hot plates. Remove the oysters from the skewers and place decoratively around the sturgeon. Slice the remaining two thirds of the mango thin and garnish each plate.

Sautéed Rainbow Trout with Swiss Chard and Chive Blossom Vinegar

Serves 4

The avid trout fisherman may say, "*What* kind of vinegar?", but this simple way of preparing a most wonderful fish adds a distinctive tartness, while the chard gives the dish a slight sweetness.

1 bunch Swiss chard
½ cup (1 stick) butter, softened and cut into pieces
1 tablespoon minced shallot
¼ cup Herb Vinegar, page 165, made with chive blossoms, or any good-quality herb vinegar
2 tablespoons heavy cream
Salt and pepper to taste
2 tablespoons clarified butter, page 165
Four 10- to 12-ounce rainbow trout

Preheat the oven to 375°. Wash the Swiss chard well and shred the leaves fine. Cut the stems into 1-inch julienne strips and set aside. In a saucepan, heat 1 teaspoon of the butter and sauté the shallot until translucent. Add the vinegar and reduce until almost dry; add the cream. Bring to a boil, reduce slightly, remove from heat, and whisk in the remaining butter in pieces. Strain, adjust the seasoning, and reserve.

Heat a heavy skillet large enough to hold the trout, or 2 smaller skillets, and add the clarified butter. Season the trout well. Brown the trout well on each side and place in the oven for 3 to 5 minutes. Remove the trout from the oven and remove the tail, head, and backbone, and, if desired, the skin. Arrange the trout on 4 preheated plates.

Reheat the skillet and toss the Swiss chard over high heat for 30 seconds, or until heated through. Season with salt and pepper. Arrange the chard on each plate along with the trout and spoon a small amount of sauce around the fillets. Serve immediately.

Sauteed Rainbow Trout with Swiss Chard and Chive Blossom Vinegar

Lamb Medallions
with Morels and Anise Hyssop

Serves 4

Northwest spring lamb and morels is a combination not to be missed. Anise hyssop, also known as licorice mint, adds a subtle distinction to this preparation. Sautéed spring peas and baby turnips make a delightful accompaniment.

Lamb Stock, page 158, Lamb Natural Juice, page 159, or
*   Brown Veal Stock, page 157*
5 anise hyssop sprigs, or 1 mint sprig and ¼ teaspoon Pernod
8 ounces fresh morels, or 1 ounce dried morels
One 1½- to 2-pound boneless lamb loin, all fat removed
Salt and pepper to taste
Peanut oil for brushing
1 teaspoon peanut oil
2 tablespoons Marsala
2 tablespoons butter

Light a wood or charcoal fire in an open grill and allow to burn down to white-red coals, or preheat the broiler. Prepare the lamb stock and strain. Place 1 of the anise hyssop sprigs in the stock; keep warm. Wash the morels well and dry on paper towels. If using dried morels, soak in cold water to cover for 15 minutes. Allow the lamb to rest at room temperature for 10 minutes. Slice the loins into 16 equal medallions, each about ½ inch thick and weighing 1½ ounces. Season with salt and pepper. Brush with oil and grill over the hottest part of the fire for 1 minute. Turn, grill for 1 minute, and remove to the warm edge of the grill. Or broil 2 inches from broiler for 1 to 2 minutes per side.

Heat a heavy skillet over high heat and, when smoking, add the 1 teaspoon peanut oil and the morels. Toss over high heat for 10 seconds. Add the Marsala, reduce to a glaze over high heat, and remove the morels from the skillet. Add ¼ cup of the lamb stock along with the infused anise hyssop sprig; reduce to a glaze. Add another ¼ cup of stock and reduce to a glaze again. Add the remaining stock and reduce over high heat until the sauce lightly coats a spoon. (If using Pernod and mint, add to the sauce now.)

Return the morels to the sauce. Swirl in the butter. Place 4 of the lamb medallions on each of preheated plates. Remove the herb sprig and spoon the morel sauce around. Garnish with the reserved anise hyssop sprigs. Serve immediately.

Roast Lamb Loin with Wild Greens
and Red Currants

Serves 4

The bright, crisp taste of lightly sautéed greens provides a refreshing contrast to the richness of Northwest lamb. Vary the greens any way you like according to what is on hand. There are many informative guides to the gathering of wild greens—or ask the old-timers in your area—and a day afield will offer many satisfying finds. Or you can buy seasonal greens in the market.

2 pieces (about 2 pounds) boneless lamb loin, trimmed of all
*   fat*
1 tablespoon plus 1 teaspoon peanut oil
4 garlic cloves
4 thyme sprigs
2 cups Lamb Stock, page 158, Lamb Natural Juice, page
*   159, or Brown Veal Stock, page 157*
1 cup fresh or frozen red currants, or 1 teaspoon currant jam

4 to 5 cups wild greens (dandelion, mâche, mizuna, arugula,
  purslane, miner's lettuce, etc.), chicory, or curly endive,
  rinsed and dried
Salt and pepper to taste
1 tablespoon balsamic vinegar
4 red currant or thyme sprigs

Preheat the oven to 400°. Cut the lamb into 4 even pieces and let sit at room temperature for 10 to 15 minutes. Heat a heavy skillet to smoking. Add 1 tablespoon of the oil and sear the lamb well on all sides. Discard the oil in the pan. Add 2 of the garlic cloves and the thyme sprigs and roast the lamb in the preheated oven for about 8 minutes (for medium rare). Meanwhile, mince the 2 remaining garlic cloves and reserve. Remove the lamb from the pan and keep warm.

Add ½ cup of the stock to the pan, scraping up any bits on the bottom of the pan, and boil to reduce to about 1 tablespoon. Add another ½ cup of stock. Add the currants or currant jam to the pan, mashing with a spoon. Reduce again to a glaze. Add the remaining 1 cup of stock and reduce until the sauce barely coats a spoon. Strain, pressing all of the liquids from the currants, and keep warm.

Heat the skillet again until smoking. Add the remaining 1 teaspoon peanut oil, the reserved minced garlic, and the greens, tossing rapidly. Season well and add the balsamic vinegar, toss again until the greens are barely wilted, and divide the greens equally among 4 plates.

Slice the lamb and arrange around the greens, garnishing with the red currant sprigs. Spoon the sauce around the lamb and serve immediately.

Hot Cherry Tarts with Rose Geranium

Serves 4

The first cherries of the season are an occasion for celebration, and this simply presented dessert is always a hit. The rose geranium—one of the edible scented geraniums, of which there are many intriguing varieties—lends a subtle, yet distinctive character.

> *Dough for Tart Crust, page 175*
> *Pastry Cream, page 177*
> *3 rose geranium leaves or your choice of scented geranium leaves, or 2 lemon verbena or mint sprigs*
> *2 pints Bing, Montmorency, or Rainier cherries*
> *2 tablespoons sugar*
> *4 small rose geranium leaves, or lemon verbena or mint sprigs, for garnish (optional)*
> *Custard, page 177, or ½ cup heavy cream, lightly whipped*

Prepare the tart dough and chill; preheat the oven to 375°. Line 4 individual tart pans with removable bottoms with the dough. Trim the dough and crimp the edges. Line the dough with parchment paper or aluminum foil, and fill with rice, beans, or pie weights. Bake the shells in the preheated oven for 5 to 8 minutes, or until lightly browned; let cool.

Prepare the pastry cream. While the cream is still warm, crush 2 of the rose geranium leaves or herb sprigs lightly and place in the cream to steep as it cools to room temperature.

Pit the cherries, reserving all of the juices. Place ½ cup of the pitted cherries, the sugar, and any reserved juices in a small saucepan and bring to a boil over low heat. Simmer for 3 minutes. Puree in a blender until completely smooth; return to the saucepan and simmer until the liquid is reduced to a shiny glaze; keep warm.

Preheat the oven to 375°. Remove the rose geranium leaves or herb sprigs from the cream and discard. Fill each of the tart shells half full with the pastry cream. Roll the remaining geranium leaf into a thin cylinder and shred it into very thin strips with a sharp knife. Divide the strips evenly among the 4 shells, blending into the cream with a small spoon. Slice the remaining pitted cherry halves into quarters and arrange the cherries attractively in the shells. Brush each tart liberally with the warm cherry glaze, being careful not to splatter it on the crusts.

Place the tarts on a baking sheet and bake for 5 to 8 minutes, or until heated through. Cover the rims of the tart shells with aluminum foil if they begin to brown too much.

Remove from the oven, garnish with rose geranium leaves or herb sprigs, if you like, and serve immediately with vanilla custard or lightly whipped cream.

Hot Cherry Tarts with Rose Geranium

Strawberry-Rhubarb Cookies

Serves 4

These lacy cookies are easy to prepare and are a new twist on an old favorite.

COOKIES
4 tablespoons butter
¼ cup brown sugar
¼ cup light corn syrup
½ cup pecans, walnuts, hazelnuts,* or almonds, minced
⅓ cup unbleached all-purpose flour

FILLING
1 cup chopped rhubarb
2 tablespoons sugar
⅛ teaspoon grated orange zest
Pinch ground ginger

CARAMEL SAUCE
2 tablespoons water
¼ cup sugar
3 tablespoons butter
3 tablespoons heavy cream

CREAM SAUCE
¾ cup heavy cream
2 tablespoons sugar
2 eggs, beaten
½ teaspoon vanilla extract

2 pints strawberries, hulled

To make the cookies   Preheat the oven to 350°. In a heavy, medium saucepan, melt the butter and stir in the brown sugar and corn syrup. Bring the mixture to a boil, stirring until the sugar dissolves. Remove from the heat and add the nuts and flour. Drop 2 tablespoonfuls of batter for each of 4 cookies onto a greased baking sheet 3 inches apart. Spread each into a circle.

Bake in the preheated oven for 8 to 10 minutes, or until lightly browned. Remove from the oven, cool for 1 minute and remove with a spatula. Form the cookies over a rolling pin and, when cool enough to handle, but still pliable, form into cones and set aside.

To make the filling   Preheat the oven to 450°. In a small baking pan, toss the rhubarb with the sugar, orange zest, and ginger and bake in the oven until tender, about 8 minutes. Let cool.

To make the caramel sauce   In a small, heavy skillet or saucepan, bring the water and sugar to a boil. Cook over medium heat without stirring until the sugar begins to caramelize. Carefully stir in the butter and, when the mixture is emulsified, add the cream, stirring carefully. Set aside and keep warm.

To make the cream sauce   In a medium saucepan, bring the cream and sugar to a boil. Whip into the beaten eggs and return this mixture to the saucepan over low heat. Stir constantly until thickened. Strain and let cool. Stir in the vanilla.

Slice half of the strawberries. Spoon the rhubarb equally into each of the 4 cones. Fill the cones with the sliced berries. Place a filled cone on each of 4 serving plates. Garnish with the remaining whole berries and spoon a small amount of the cream sauce and the caramel sauce around each cone. Serve immediately.

*If using hazelnuts, place in an ovenproof skillet and toast in a preheated 350° oven for 6 to 8 minutes. Let cool, then rub the skins off in a towel or with the palms of your hands.

SUMMER

SUMMER

There are children in the meadow with pails full of blackberries, their faces and shirts deep purple, berry-stained smiles brightening their faces.

There in the mountains,
There you feel free
T. S. Eliot

Time stands still during summer in the Pacific Northwest. Storms blow through from the turbulent coast, and autumn's snap seems always to come too quickly. Yet there remain those days when raspberries hang corpulently, coral and green-blue-backed salmon are landed in straining nets, steaming orange-red Dungeness crabs are piled high on picnic tables, and berries, nectarines, and peaches fill kitchens with heady fragrance—and the deep blue skies open wider and wider. With the backdrop of the snow-capped peaks, Mts. Rainier, Baker, Adams, and Hood, the Cascades and the Olympics, a meal as simple as salmon roasted with herbs, lightly dressed summer greens, and peaches and nectarines is timeless and exquisite.

To dine with a glacier on a sunny day is a glorious thing and
makes common feasts of meat and wine ridiculous. The glacier
eats hills and drinks sunbeams. John Muir

Summer means seafood, and the calendar is marked by the arrival of the first halibut, Bristol Bay sockeye salmon, coastal king salmon, Dungeness crab, Hood Canal shrimp, and crayfish and trout from the inland rivers.

There are few greater pleasures than the aroma of seafood baking over a driftwood fire. The cooking of the Pacific Northwest was born in this wood smoke and sea air, and we continue to create new foods, new tastes, inspired by this setting.

The thought of summer in the Northwest brings smiles to natives and newcomers alike, and the cook is overwhelmed with the variety, quality, and quantity of superb vegetables and fruits. It is especially enjoyable to prepare dishes combining many varieties of vegetables, whether as appetizers, garnishes to main courses, or as light entrees. Fruits, too, come to the fore as bright accompaniments to grilled meats and poultry. Summer samplers of fruits and berries capture the love of summer in all of us. Cobblers, pies, and tarts—crisp, warm, and tangy, and cooled with the richness of fresh ice cream—will be remembered long after the sun-washed days have passed.

I am always glad to touch the living rock again . . . and dip my
head in the high mountain sky. John Muir

The pleasure of summer cooking is its casual simplicity and lightness, the gathering of friends around the fire and the picnic table, the tasks of pitting cherries, cleaning crab, preserving fruits, making jams or pickles.

The following recipes from the summer in the Pacific Northwest will help you create new dishes to celebrate this season.

Summer Recipes

Ahi with Fennel, Cucumbers, and Columbia River Caviar

Summer Vegetables with Fontina

Chilled Dungeness Crab with Sea Beans, Chicory, and Dill Vinaigrette

Peppered Mango and Iced Hood Canal Shrimp

Marinated Squid and Octopus Salad with Tomatoes, Sorrel, and Achiote

Goat Cheese and Zucchini Gratin with Lentils and Smoked Tomato Coulis

Crayfish and Spot Prawn Minestrone with Dungeness Crab Ravioli

Halibut Breaded with Hazelnuts and Lemon Verbena Sauce

Smoked Trout with Walla Walla Onions and Corn Relish

Grilled Coho Salmon with Sugar Snap Peas and Corn

King Salmon Roasted with Thyme, Tarragon, and Fennel

Marinated Grilled Chicken with Artichokes, Eggplant, and Oregano

Spit-roasted Chicken with Cherry Chutney

Chilled Veal Loin with Summer Salad and Cucumber Coulis

Northwest Summer Pudding

Peach and Nectarine Gratin with Raspberry Coulis

Hot Figs and Apricots with Mirabelle Plum Ice Cream

Blueberry Cobbler with Orange Custard

Peach Crisp with Blackberry Sauce

Summer Preserves

Ahi with Fennel, Cucumbers, and Columbia River Caviar

Serves 4

To attempt to embellish perfection would be foolhardy. Ahi, or yellowfin tuna from Hawaii, is prized for sashimi and, when combined with caviar from the Columbia River, makes a truly exquisite dish.

2 ounces Columbia River or other high-quality caviar
8 ounces sashimi-grade ahi, albacore, bluefin, marlin, or
*   swordfish*
2 English cucumbers
1 fennel bulb
Extra-virgin olive oil for tossing

Chill the caviar, ahi, and 4 serving plates. Peel the cucumbers and reserve one half of a cucumber. Slice the remaining 1½ cucumbers lengthwise very thinly. Reserve 8 of the most attractive slices. Tightly roll the remaining slices lengthwise and slice the rolls thinly. Immerse in ice water. Cut the reserved half cucumber and the fennel into julienne, reserving a few fennel sprigs for garnish; set aside.

Slice the tuna into 12 very thin slices. Arrange 2 slices on each chilled plate. Place each remaining slice in the palm of your hand and cup it in your hand to form a pocket. Place the pockets behind the slices on each plate. Toss the cucumber and fennel julienne and arrange in each pocket. Remove the shredded cucumber from the ice water and drain well. Toss lightly with a few drops of olive oil and arrange behind the slices. Spoon a small amount of caviar onto each plate. Garnish with the reserved fennel sprigs and, if not served immediately, chill well.

Summer Vegetables with Fontina

Serves 4

This dish bursts with luscious flavors when tomatoes are at their ripest, making an excellent appetizer, a beautiful light lunch, or a summer supper. Choose the ripest, juiciest vine-ripened tomatoes you can find. The tomatoes should be served at room temperature, the vegetables chilled, and the fontina hot for a dipping sauce.

4 ripe medium tomatoes
12 to 16 asparagus spears
4 to 8 baby zucchini (about 2 inches long), or 1 medium
*   zucchini cut with a melon baller*
8 small carrots (about 2 inches long), with tops, or 2
*   medium carrots cut in 1½-inch-long diagonals*
1 cup sugar snap peas, or ¾ cup shelled peas
4 to 8 baby artichokes
1 cup grated fontina cheese, or any good-quality white
*   melting cheese such as Gruyère, Bel Paese, mozzarella, or*
*   Cougar Gold Cheddar*

Ahi with Fennel, Cucumbers, and Columbia River Caviar

1 ½ teaspoons minced shallots
½ cup extra-virgin olive oil
3 tablespoons freshly squeezed lemon juice
Salt and pepper to taste
8 ounces chanterelles, shiitakes, oyster mushrooms, or other
*   wild mushrooms*
1 tablespoon Marsala

Core the tomatoes and cut a ¾-inch-deep bowl in the top of each. Set aside at room temperature. Trim 1 inch from the bottom of the asparagus. Blanch each kind of vegetable except the mushrooms separately in boiling salted water in turn until crisp-tender, finishing with the artichokes. Drain and immerse each in ice water; set aside. Trim the tough outer leaves and stems from the artichokes and cut in half lengthwise.

Melt the fontina slowly in a saucepan over boiling water, stirring until very smooth; set aside and keep warm. In a small saucepan, sauté the shallots in 1 teaspoon of the olive oil until translucent; add the lemon juice. Whisk in all but 1 teaspoon of the remaining olive oil, remove from the heat, and whisk until the sauce is emulsified. Adjust the seasoning and set aside.

In a large skillet, sauté the wild mushrooms in the remaining 1 teaspoon olive oil for 30 seconds. Add the Marsala and boil to reduce to a glaze. Add the blanched vegetables and sauté until heated through, about 1 minute. Remove from heat and let cool. Add the reserved lemon and olive oil mixture, adjust the seasoning, and refrigerate for 2 hours.

Preheat the broiler. Season the tomatoes with salt and pepper. Spoon the fontina into each tomato and glaze lightly under the broiler. Place a tomato in the center of each of 4 room-temperature plates and arrange the marinated vegetables attractively around it. Serve immediately.

Chilled Dungeness Crab with Sea Beans, Chicory, and Dill Vinaigrette

Chilled Dungeness Crab with Sea Beans, Chicory, and Dill Vinaigrette

Serves 4

In the Northwest a small boat and a few crab pots mean contentment. This simple preparation captures the essence of summer on the water. Sea beans, from a crisp, grasslike plant called salnicornia that thrives in salt marshes, give a unique sea taste to this salad.

> *2 tablespoons crab boil flavoring (optional)*
> *10 to 12 ounces cooked fresh Dungeness crab meat, or two 2½-pound live crabs*
> *4 ounces sea beans, green beans, asparagus, or snow peas*
> *1 head chicory or curly endive*
> *Basic Vinaigrette, page 165, with ½ teaspoon minced fresh dill*
> *4 dill sprigs for garnish*
> *1 ripe tomato cut into 8 wedges*

If using live crabs, add the crab boil to a large pot filled with water and bring to a rolling boil. Plunge in the live crabs, turn off the heat, and let sit, covered, for five minutes. Stir, cover, and allow to sit 1 minute. Remove the crabs and immerse them in ice water until thoroughly chilled, about 5 minutes. Refrigerate.

If using green beans or asparagus, cut them into 2-inch lengths and blanch in boiling water until crisp-tender; drain and immerse in ice water. Wash the chicory and dry it well. If using whole crabs, clean and shell the crabs (a mallet and a nut pick work well), reserving the shells to use for stock and the orange-colored "butter" to add to butter sauces or soups.

Toss the chicory and sea beans or another vegetable very lightly in a small amount of vinaigrette and arrange in the center of each of 4 plates. Arrange one-fourth of the crab meat on top and spoon more vinaigrette around. Garnish with the dill and tomato wedges.

Peppered Mango and Iced Hood Canal Shrimp

Serves 4

This is once-a-year bliss, when mangoes are succulent and juicy and the local Hood Canal spot shrimp run in early July. You can purchase the shrimp raw or cooked. If raw, simply poach lightly in salted water and chill. Prawns or crayfish are good alternatives, but nothing compares to the taste of these Hood Canal treasures.

> *2 mangoes*
> *1 teaspoon black peppercorns*
> *Court Bouillon, page 166*
> *3 pounds Hood Canal shrimp, Gulf prawns, or crayfish in the shell*
> *Basic Vinaigrette, page 165*

Peel and seed the mangoes, reserving all the juice for another use (see page 179). Chill the mangoes thoroughly and slice thin. Crush the peppercorns fine with a mallet or cleaver.

Place the court bouillon in a large saucepan and bring to a boil. Plunge the shrimp in, turn off the heat, stir well, and poach for 2 minutes. Drain and immerse in ice water; drain and chill.

Prepare the vinaigrette. Arrange the mango slices on each of 4 chilled plates. Sprinkle some of the crushed peppercorns over the mango slices, if desired. Arrange the chilled shrimp equally among the plates. Add the crushed peppercorns to the vinaigrette, spoon a small amount around the mango slices, and serve immediately.

Marinated Squid and Octopus Salad with Tomatoes, Sorrel, and Achiote

Serves 4

This stunning salad tastes even better than it looks. Achiote—the seed of the annatto tree, used extensively in Caribbean cuisine—is sweet, musky, and bright, an explosive combination with tart sorrel and luscious vine-ripened tomatoes. Be sure to cook the octopus and squid very briefly, and serve the dish chilled.

1 to 1½ pounds small squid
8 ounces octopus tentacles, preferably small
2 cups dry white wine
2 thyme sprigs
½ onion
2 cloves
2 bay leaves
3 tablespoons vinegar
Basic Vinaigrette, page 165
1 teaspoon minced fresh oregano
1 teaspoon minced fresh parsley
Salt and fresh-ground black pepper to taste
1 bunch sorrel or spinach
1 teaspoon achiote seeds, crushed (available at Mexican markets)
2 tablespoons heavy cream
4 medium ripe tomatoes

Clean the squid by running it under cold water, peeling off the outer membrane, and removing the viscera in the tubes. Cut the eyes and beak from the tentacles and reserve the tentacles. Rinse well. Slice the tubes ¼ inch thick. Slice the octopus tentacles as thin as possible.

In a non-aluminum saucepan, simmer the white wine, thyme, onion, cloves, bay leaves, and vinegar for 5 minutes; strain. Return the mixture to the saucepan and bring to a simmer. Plunge the squid into the poaching mixture, stir, and remove. Repeat the procedure with the octopus.

Prepare the vinaigrette. While the squid and octopus are still warm, toss with 3 tablespoons of the vinaigrette, the oregano and parsley, and salt and pepper. Let cool, then refrigerate for 2 hours or overnight.

Wash and dry the sorrel or spinach. Remove the center stem of the sorrel or spinach leaves and roll the leaves like a cigar; shred the roll finely and set aside.

Combine the achiote and cream in a small saucepan. Bring to a boil and simmer for 3 minutes, or until bright orange in color. Add the cream to the remaining vinaigrette in a blender and blend on low speed for 5 minutes to bring out the flavor of the achiote; strain. Slice the tomatoes and arrange in a circle on each of 4 chilled plates. Place a small nest of the sorrel in the center. Toss the squid and octopus and place attractively in the center of the sorrel. Serve immediately.

Marinated Squid and Octopus Salad with Tomatoes, Sorrel, and Achiote

Goat Cheese and Zucchini Gratin
with Lentils and Smoked Tomato Coulis

Serves 4

There are many rich, flavorful goat cheeses produced on small farms in the Cascades and in the Chehalis area of Washington, and in the dairy regions of coastal Oregon. The rich, nutty flavor of goat cheese is the centerpiece of this fragrant dish, combined with the earthy smoothness of zucchini and lentils. The smoked tomato adds a surprising, piquant finish.

¾ cup dried lentils
8 ounces soft-ripened cream-type goat cheese such as Mt.
  Capra, Quilliscant, Sally Jackson, or Montrachet
1 medium zucchini
2 garlic cloves
2 teaspoons olive oil
1 tablespoon minced onion
1 tablespoon minced pancetta or bacon
1 bay leaf
Salt and pepper to taste
2 cups Chicken Stock, page 158, or canned chicken broth
Basic Vinaigrette, page 165
2 tablespoons fine bread crumbs
1 tablespoon minced fresh chives
⅓ cup extra-virgin olive oil
1 teaspoon minced fresh parsley
⅛ teaspoon minced fresh thyme
8 to 12 lettuce leaves
Smoked Tomato Coulis, recipe following

Soak the lentils in cold water to cover for 1 hour. Cut the goat cheese into 1-inch-thick pieces and refrigerate. Slice the zucchini lengthwise into 8 thin slices. Mince 1 of the garlic cloves. Heat a heavy skillet over high heat and, when smoking, add 1 teaspoon of the olive oil. Add the zucchini strips and sauté over high heat until well browned; turn carefully, browning the other side, and add the minced garlic. Remove the pan from the heat, allowing the garlic to toast lightly. Remove the zucchini slices to paper towels and let cool.

In a medium saucepan, sauté the onion with the pancetta or bacon until translucent. Add the soaked lentils, the toasted garlic and the bay leaf and season with salt and pepper. Add the chicken stock. Bring to a boil and simmer for 15 to 20 minutes, or until the lentils are tender. Drain. Toss with 3 tablespoons of the vinaigrette and allow to cool to room temperature.

Preheat the oven to 400°. Wrap each piece of goat cheese diagonally with a browned zucchini slice. Wrap the sides of each piece with another slice, trimming evenly. Combine the bread crumbs and minced chives and sprinkle lightly over the top of the cheeses. Place the wrapped cheeses on an ovenproof platter or baking dish, drizzle with the ⅓ cup olive oil, and bake in the preheated oven for approximately 5 minutes, or until the cheese is heated through, but still firm.

Mince the remaining garlic clove. Toss the lentils with the minced parsley, thyme, and garlic and arrange in the lettuce leaves on each of 4 plates. Remove the cheese from the oven, brown under the broiler if desired, and divide among the plates. Spoon a small amount of the coulis around each piece of cheese and serve immediately.

SMOKED TOMATO COULIS
1 ripe tomato
Salt and freshly ground black pepper to taste
1 to 2 tablespoons olive oil
Chicken Stock, page 158, or canned chicken broth for
  thinning (optional)
Fresh lemon juice to taste

Plunge the tomato into boiling water for 10 seconds, then immerse it in ice water. Peel, cut in half, and remove seeds. Season with salt and pepper and cold-smoke for 15 to 20 minutes as described on page 163, or grill under a broiler until browned. Puree in a blender or food processor until very smooth, then add the olive oil in a thin stream. Adjust the consistency with chicken stock if necessary, and season with salt, pepper, and lemon juice.

Crayfish and Spot Prawn Minestrone with Dungeness Crab Ravioli

Serves 4

This is an unforgettable soup. Although it is involved, it can be prepared in stages and is very satisfying. Make extra ravioli while you're at it. They are wonderful simply prepared in butter and herbs. The stock also makes a superb base for sauces. This main-course soup is perfect in any season—just vary the vegetables accordingly.

STOCK
½ leek
½ carrot
1 small onion
½ cup chopped mushrooms
1 celery stalk
2 tarragon sprigs
2 basil leaves
1 thyme sprig
2 oregano sprigs
4 garlic cloves
2 teaspoons olive oil
2 to 3 quarts crushed crab, crayfish, lobster, or shrimp shells
   (available from your fish merchant)
¼ cup cognac or brandy, heated
2 cups dry white wine
6 ripe tomatoes, quartered
2 tablespoons tomato paste
2 bay leaves
2 to 3 quarts Fish Stock, page 157, or bottled clam juice

4 to 8 large spot or Gulf prawns
24 crayfish

RAVIOLI
Pasta Dough, page 172
½ cup whole-milk ricotta
1 teaspoon minced fresh parsley
1 teaspoon minced fresh basil
1 garlic clove, minced
1 egg yolk
Lemon juice to taste
3 ounces fresh cooked Dungeness crab meat
Salt and pepper to taste
Semolina flour for dusting

GARNISH
¼ cup dried white beans, soaked for 1 to 2 hours or
   overnight
1 tablespoon olive oil
½ cup cut-up green beans
¼ cup julienne-cut leek
¼ cup julienne-cut carrot
¼ cup julienne-cut celery
¼ cup julienne-cut fennel
2 large tomatoes, peeled, seeded, and diced
½ cup chanterelles, cèpes, morels, shiitakes, or oyster
   mushrooms
4 basil leaves, finely shredded
1 tablespoon mixed minced fresh tarragon, parsley, and
   oregano
2 garlic cloves, minced

Crayfish and Spot Prawn Minestrone with Dungeness Crab Ravioli

To make the stock   Coarsely chop all the vegetables, herbs, and garlic. Heat the olive oil in an 8- to 10-quart saucepan, add the vegetables, herbs, and garlic, and sauté over low heat for about 15 minutes. Add the shells, raise the heat to high, and sauté for 5 minutes, breaking the shells with a wooden spoon. Add the cognac and light with a match to flame. Boil to reduce by half and add the wine, tomatoes, tomato paste, and bay leaves. Bring to a boil. Add 2 quarts of the fish stock. Simmer for 2 hours, skimming frequently, adding more fish stock if necessary.

Place the spot prawns and crayfish in a strainer and immerse in the stock; when the shells turn red, remove and immerse in ice water. Peel the prawns and add the shells to the stock. Peel the crayfish tails and add the shells to the stock, reserving the heads for garnish, if desired. Reserve the prawn and crayfish meat. Strain the stock and reduce to about 1½ quarts if necessary.

To make the ravioli   Prepare the pasta dough. Combine the ricotta, herbs, garlic, egg yolk, and lemon juice in a small bowl. Fold in the crab meat carefully without making a paste. Season with salt and pepper. Roll the pasta into 2 thin, almost transparent sheets. Spoon out the filling on 1 sheet to make 8 ravioli, or 4 larger ones. Brush the edges of the dough lightly with water and cover with the second sheet of dough. Press lightly to seal the edges, and cut with a knife or ravioli cutter. Dust with semolina flour and cover with a dry towel or waxed paper and refrigerate for 15 to 20 minutes.

To make the garnish   Simmer the white beans in salted water for 15 to 20 minutes or until tender; set aside. Blanch the green beans for 3 to 5 minutes. In a skillet, heat the olive oil and sauté all the remaining vegetables and mushrooms until crisp-tender.

Cook the ravioli in a large amount of slowly boiling salted water until al dente, about 8 minutes; drain. Add the vegetables and beans to the stock. Bring to a simmer, add the shellfish, return to a simmer, and add the ravioli. Add the herbs and minced garlic. Divide the ravioli and garnish among 4 heated wide-rim soup bowls and ladle the stock over. Serve immediately.

Halibut Breaded with Hazelnuts and Lemon Verbena Sauce

Serves 4

While salmon is the king of the Northwest, halibut from the Pacific, especially the cold Alaskan waters, is a rich, flavorful, meaty-textured fish that many prefer. The nut mixture in this recipe seals in the juices and adds a unique taste and texture to the fish, a technique that can be adapted to prepare any white-flaked fish. Be sure to coat the fish carefully, so that the breading does not become heavy. Baby yellow squash and whole braised red onions make a delightful accompaniment.

Lemon verbena is a delightful herb that grows profusely in the Northwest, is perfect with any type of seafood or fowl, and is also good in sorbets, ice creams, and desserts. I grow an abundance every summer and pack it in peanut oil. It will keep refrigerated for months—just remove it from the oil and use as if it were fresh—and the resulting oil makes a fine vinaigrette.

½ cup hazelnuts

SAUCE
Vin Blanc Sauce, page 162
1½ tablespoons minced fresh lemon verbena leaves, or 1
*   teaspoon fresh lemon juice*
1 parsley sprig
3 tablespoons butter, softened
Salt and pepper to taste
Four 6-ounce halibut fillets, skin removed
2 tablespoons peanut oil

Preheat the oven to 350°. Place the hazelnuts in an ovenproof skillet and toast in the preheated oven for 6 to 8 minutes. Let cool, then rub the skins off in a towel or with the palms of your hands. Grind the hazelnuts very fine in a blender, food proces-

sor, or nut grinder. Place the ground hazelnuts on a baking sheet or large plate and set aside.

To make the sauce, prepare the Vin Blanc Sauce and cool to tepid. Puree in a blender with the lemon verbena, parsley, and butter; strain. Adjust the seasoning and keep warm.

Season the halibut fillets and lightly press the top side into the hazelnut mixture, being sure to cover the entire surface of the fish without mashing the breading.

Preheat the oven to 375°. If you have a skillet large enough to hold all 4 fillets without crowding, heat the peanut oil until hot but not smoking and add the halibut fillets. When evenly browned, after about 1 minute, turn the fillets over and place the skillet in the upper rack of the oven. If you need to use 2 skillets, follow the same procedure with 2 fillets in each skillet. The fish will take about 4 minutes to bake. Remove the fish to paper towels and then onto heated plates. Spoon the sauce around the fish.

Smoked Trout with Walla Walla Onions and Corn Relish

Serves 4

A perfect picnic dish to enjoy on a soft, warm summer day, or to serve as a light evening meal at sunset. Easily prepared, this dish benefits from a day of refrigeration to allow the flavors to blend. Walla Walla onions are sweet and mild, with a fresh taste all their own.

2 fresh whole trout, approximately 10 ounces each, boned, or
*   4 smoked trout fillets*
2 medium Walla Walla or Vidalia onions

³/₄ cup cider vinegar
1 tablespoon sugar, or to taste
¹/₃ cup dry white wine
¹/₃ cup water
1 tablespoon minced onion
¹/₈ teaspoon ground ginger
Pinch ground allspice
Pinch dried red pepper flakes
1 teaspoon cornstarch dissolved in 2 teaspoons water
2 tablespoons raisins
1 ear sweet corn, or about 1¹/₂ cups corn kernels
2 tablespoons minced red bell pepper
1 teaspoon minced fresh parsley
1 teaspoon minced fresh chives
¹/₈ teaspoon minced fresh rosemary
Salt and pepper to taste
4 lettuce leaves
¹/₄ cup Basic Vinaigrette, page 165

Brine and smoke the fresh trout as described on page 152, smoking 4 slices of a Walla Walla onion along with the trout for the final 15 minutes. If you are using smoked trout, grill the onion slices under a broiler until browned. Let cool to room temperature and refrigerate.

Bring the vinegar, sugar, white wine, water, minced onion, and dried spices to a boil in a small, non-aluminum saucepan. Simmer for 2 to 3 minutes, then thicken lightly with the cornstarch dissolved in water. Add the raisins and set the mixture aside to cool to room temperature.

Blanch the corn on the cob for 2 minutes in rapidly boiling water. Immerse in cold water and drain. Scrape the kernels from the corn cob and add the corn to the cooled spiced liquid, stirring well to blend. Add the diced pepper and minced herbs and season with salt and pepper. Refrigerate along with the trout for at least 2 hours, or overnight if desired.

To serve, remove the head, tail, and skin from the trout and carefully remove the fillets, allowing 1 fillet per person. Place 1 of the smoked onion slices on each of 4 chilled plates and place a trout fillet on top. Place a lettuce leaf on each of the 4 plates and fill with a large spoonful of the corn relish. Slice the remaining Walla Walla onions thinly and separate 2 of the slices into rings. Place the rings decoratively around the corn relish. Dress the onions with the vinaigrette and serve immediately.

Grilled Coho Salmon
with Sugar Snap Peas and Corn

Serves 4

After the final king salmon run of late summer, the cohos, or silver salmon, arrive in the coastal and inland waters. Firm and bright red in color, these fish are exceptionally well flavored and buttery. Including the season's peak of corn and snap peas, this dish makes a perfect meal to celebrate the joys of summer.

1 ear sweet corn
1 cup sugar snap peas, or ¾ cup shelled peas
Four 6-ounce coho fillets
Peanut oil for brushing
Salt and pepper to taste
6 tablespoons butter, softened
⅛ teaspoon minced fresh thyme
1 teaspoon minced fresh chives
½ teaspoon minced fresh parsley

Prepare a wood or charcoal fire in an open grill, or preheat the broiler. Shuck the corn and scrape the kernels off the cob with a sharp knife.

Shell half of the peas (or, if the pods are small enough, slice thinly on the bias).

When the coals are white, brush the fillets with oil, season, and grill for 3 minutes over the hottest part of the fire. Turn, brush with oil, and move to the side of the fire until the fillets are barely opaque in the center, about 3 to 5 minutes. Or grill for 3 minutes on each side under the broiler.

Heat 1 tablespoon of the butter in a small skillet and, when it is foamy, add the pea pods, shelled peas, and corn. Season and toss until tender, about 1 minute. Remove from the heat, add the minced herbs, and slowly add the remaining 5 tablespoons of butter, swirling the pan gently. Adjust the seasoning. Spoon the sauce equally onto 4 plates. Lay 1 salmon fillet on each plate and garnish with the sautéed vegetables. Serve immediately.

King Salmon Roasted with Thyme,
Tarragon, and Fennel

Serves 4

I must have prepared this dish hundreds of times over the past few years, yet I have never grown tired of it. I believe it is the perfect way to prepare king salmon. And everyone who has tasted it agrees! Rex Hill, a superb Pinot Noir from the Willamette Valley of Oregon, is excellent in this sauce, as is any good-quality Pinot Noir. Cabernet Sauvignon, Petite Syrah, and full-bodied Bordeaux and Burgundies are also suitable. New potatoes roasted in butter, and the best vegetables of the season, simply prepared, are the best accompaniments.

SAUCE
2 shallots, minced
⅓ cup chopped mushrooms

1 sprig each tarragon, thyme, and fennel
1 tablespoon peanut oil
⅔ cup red wine vinegar, preferably Kimberly Cabernet
1 cup Pinot Noir wine
2 tablespoons heavy cream
½ cup (1 stick) butter, softened
Salt, pepper, and fresh lemon juice to taste

SALMON
Salt and pepper to taste
Four 6-ounce salmon fillets, skin on, at room temperature
4 tarragon sprigs
4 thyme sprigs
½ cup chopped fennel
4 tablespoons butter
1 tablespoon peanut oil

Preheat the oven to 400°. To prepare the sauce, sauté the shallots, mushrooms, tarragon, thyme, and fennel in the peanut oil until the shallots are translucent. Add the vinegar and boil to reduce by two thirds. Add the wine and reduce until the liquid is almost completely evaporated and the vegetables begin to caramelize. Add the cream and reduce until thickened. Remove from the heat and whip in the softened butter in small amounts. Strain through a fine sieve, pressing out all liquid. Adjust the seasoning with salt, pepper, and lemon juice; set aside and keep warm.

Salt and pepper the flesh side of each salmon fillet. With a sharp knife, peel the skin back from the fillets and place 1 tarragon sprig, 1 thyme sprig, 2 tablespoons fennel, and 1 tablespoon butter on each salmon fillet. Place the skin over the herbs and butter. Heat a cast iron or other heavy ovenproof skillet and, when it is very hot, add the oil, then the salmon, flesh side down. Brown the salmon well. Bake in the preheated oven until the fish is just opaque in the center, about 5 to 7 minutes.

To serve, remove the skin and herbs from the salmon. Spoon the sauce onto 4 heated plates, place the salmon on the sauce, and serve immediately.

Marinated Grilled Chicken
with Artichokes, Eggplant, and Oregano

Serves 4

A wonderful way to grill chicken for a summer barbecue. It's a good idea to prepare extra artichokes, as they are delicious with a dip made from the roasted eggplant puree.

7 garlic cloves
½ cup olive oil
¼ cup peanut oil
4 tarragon sprigs
4 thyme sprigs
3 parsley sprigs
1 rosemary sprig
2 oregano sprigs
1 teaspoon black peppercorns, crushed and tied in cheesecloth
4 chicken breasts, boned and skinned (about 6 ounces each)
24 baby artichokes, or 8 medium artichokes
Juice from 2 lemons
½ large eggplant
Olive oil for brushing
½ to 1 cup Chicken Stock, page 158, or canned chicken broth
2 tablespoons heavy cream
2 tablespoons butter
Salt and pepper to taste

Crush 4 of the garlic cloves. In a small saucepan, heat the oils over low heat to about 110°, and add the crushed garlic to the oils along with the herbs and peppercorns (reserving 1 oregano sprig). Remove from the heat and let cool to room temperature. Place the chicken breasts in a non-aluminum container just large enough to hold them snugly and pour the oil mixture over them.

Allow the chicken to marinate at room temperature for up to

King Salmon Roasted with Thyme, Tarragon, and Fennel

30 minutes while you prepare the garnish and the sauce. Bring a large pot of salted water to a boil. Add the artichokes and boil until a leaf can be removed easily from the center (about 10 minutes for baby artichokes and about 25 to 30 minutes for larger ones). Drain and immerse immediately in ice water; when thoroughly cooled, remove.

Clean the artichokes by removing the tough outer leaves and stem; cut them in half lengthwise and remove the hairy choke. Reserve 12 attractive leaves for garnish. (The baby artichokes may be simply cut in half lengthwise; trim off the top of each one with a knife.) Slice the artichoke bottoms into attractive triangles or julienne. Brush with lemon juice and set aside. (Reserve any trimmings for another use.)

Light a wood or charcoal fire in an open grill. Preheat the oven to 400°. Cut a 1-inch-wide strip of skin from the eggplant, leaving ½ inch of flesh on the strip. Cut this strip into ¾-inch diamond shapes or squares and toss lightly in ½ teaspoon of the lemon juice; set aside. Brush the eggplant with olive oil and roast in the preheated oven until evenly browned. Return the eggplant to the oven with the remaining 3 garlic cloves and continue roasting, turning occasionally, until the eggplant and garlic are evenly well browned. Remove from the oven and, when cool enough to handle, remove the remaining skin and discard. Puree the eggplant in a blender or food processor until very smooth (about 5 minutes). You should have about 1 cup of puree. Add the chicken stock, cream, and 6 to 8 leaves of oregano to ½ cup eggplant puree and blend until smooth, adding more chicken stock if necessary to make a smooth light sauce. (Reserve the remaining puree for other uses, such as chilled vegetable dip.) Adjust seasoning.

When the fire has burned down to white-red coals, remove the chicken breasts from the marinade and wipe off the excess oil. Grill the breasts 4 to 6 minutes on one side, being careful not to blacken, turn, and grill 4 to 6 minutes to one side of the fire, brushing lightly with the reserved marinade. Chicken may also be broiled for 4 to 6 minutes on each side, 3 to 4 inches from the broiler heating element.

Mince the remaining oregano leaves. Melt the butter in a medium skillet and, when foamy, add the artichoke garnish (or baby artichokes) and the eggplant garnish. Sauté until heated through (about 15 seconds), and season with salt and pepper. Sprinkle with some of the minced oregano.

Slice the chicken breasts on the bias and fan out on 4 preheated plates. Spoon the artichokes and eggplant decoratively around the slices, add the minced oregano to the eggplant sauce, and spoon around the chicken. Serve immediately.

Spit-roasted Chicken with Cherry Chutney

Serves 4

From May to July, baskets all over the Northwest are brimming with luscious, ripe cherries. Once you have eaten your fill of pies, tarts, cobblers, ice cream, and juicy handfuls, try this chicken with cherry chutney. The chutney is tangy and naturally sweet, and is also wonderful with pork and game. Corn on the cob is a natural accompaniment to this dish, as are buttered green beans, coleslaw, and hot biscuits.

CHERRY CHUTNEY
1 pound ripe cherries
¼ cup red wine vinegar
1½ cups Cabernet Sauvignon or Pinot Noir wine, or any
good-quality dry red wine
2 tablespoons brown sugar
1 cinnamon stick
⅛ teaspoon coriander seeds, crushed
2 whole cloves
Juice of ½ orange
1 teaspoon fresh-grated orange zest

2 thyme sprigs and ¼ teaspoon black peppercorns, crushed,
*   tied in a cheesecloth bag*
1 teaspoon cornstarch mixed with 1 teaspoon water

2 whole frying chickens, 2½ to 3 pounds each
Juice of 2 lemons
Salt and pepper to taste
2 thyme sprigs
Peanut oil for brushing

To prepare the chutney, pit the cherries, reserving all the juice. In a non-aluminum saucepan, combine the reserved juice, vinegar, wine, brown sugar, spices, orange juice and zest, and bag of herbs; and bring to a boil. Simmer the mixture slowly for 5 minutes and thicken by whisking in a few drops of the cornstarch mixture. Strain into a non-aluminum container and cool to room temperature. Add the cherries and allow them to steep for 2 hours or overnight for the flavors to blend and mellow. Remove the cheesecloth bag and discard.

Prepare a wood or charcoal fire in an open grill with a rotisserie and let it burn down to white-red coals. Plum, cherry, apple, pear, or alder are the best woods to use. Try placing a few green pieces of wood on the fire for the last few minutes. Rub the chickens all over with the lemon juice. Salt and pepper the chicken on all sides and in the body cavity. Place a thyme sprig inside each chicken. Allow to sit at room temperature for 15 minutes before placing on the rotisserie. Trim off all excess fat, truss the legs tightly onto the rotisserie, and cook slowly 10 to 12 inches from the fire for 30 to 45 minutes. It is best to move the coals to the side of the chickens so that they are cooked by reflective heat, not directly over the coals.

Lower the chickens on the rotisserie 3 inches. Mix 2 parts peanut oil with the remaining lemon juice and brush the chickens with it; continue to roast for another 30 minutes. Lower the chickens to 4 inches from the fire and roast for another 10 to 15 minutes, or until the birds are evenly browned, being careful to extinguish any flare-ups in the fire.

Remove the birds from the grill and allow them to rest for 10

minutes in a warm place. Remove from the rotisserie and disjoint the birds, first separating the legs from the carcass, and then removing the breast. Serve immediately, garnishing the plates with a small amount of chutney.

Note   The cooking time may vary, according to the heat of the fire and the age of the chicken. The chicken is done when juices run clear when the flesh is pierced with a skewer at the thigh joint.

Chilled Veal Loin with Summer Salad and Cucumber Coulis

Serves 4

This is a perfect dish for summer entertaining, as all the preparation may be done well ahead of time and easily finished at the last minute. The veal is also delicious served hot, accompanied with sautéed eggplant and zucchini. And the cucumber coulis is a refreshing highlight to any salad.

1 pound boneless veal loin
Salt and pepper to taste
2 teaspoons peanut oil
1 teaspoon minced fresh oregano
2 teaspoons minced fresh parsley
2 teaspoons minced fresh basil
1 teaspoon minced fresh chives
1 teaspoon minced fresh rosemary
2 teaspoons white peppercorns, crushed
2 teaspoons mustard seeds, crushed
2 garlic cloves, minced
2 teaspoons butter, softened

4 to 6 cups salad greens such as mizuna, arugula, chicory,
  Bibb lettuce, green leaf lettuce, oak leaf lettuce,
  purslane, miner's lettuce

CUCUMBER COULIS
2 cucumbers
1 tablespoon wine vinegar
1 tablespoon sour cream (or yogurt)
Salt and pepper to taste
Juice of 1 lemon
⅓ cup peanut oil

Basic Vinaigrette, page 165
2 to 3 small ripe tomatoes, sliced

Preheat the oven to 450°. Trim the loin of all fat and silver skin. Salt and pepper well. Heat a heavy skillet with the peanut oil and brown the loin well on all sides. Roast the loin in the preheated oven for 5 to 8 minutes, or until rare. In a small bowl, combine the herbs, peppercorns, mustard seeds, and garlic. Remove the veal from the oven and place on a cooling rack or inverted plate. When cooled, rub the veal with the softened butter and coat it well with the herb mixture. Return the roast to the oven for 5 to 8 minutes, or until medium rare, or longer if desired. Refrigerate the loin for 3 to 4 hours or overnight.

Wash the greens well; dry and refrigerate. To make the coulis, slice 1 of the unpeeled cucumbers into ½-inch-thick slices; chop coarsely and puree in a blender or food processor for 1 minute. Pour the puree into a fine sieve lined with a kitchen towel and allow to drain for 5 minutes. Lightly squeeze out any remaining liquid. Return the puree to the blender or food processor; puree again and repeat the draining process. Return to the blender or food processor. Add the vinegar, sour cream, salt and pepper, and a light squeeze of lemon. Blend on high speed and add the peanut oil in a thin stream. Blend until completely emulsified and smooth; refrigerate.

Toss the salad greens lightly with vinaigrette. Peel and thinly slice the remaining cucumber. Arrange the greens decoratively on 4 chilled plates, garnishing with the sliced cucumber and the tomatoes. Slice the veal loin thinly and arrange around the greens. Spoon a small amount of the coulis around the greens and serve immediately.

Chilled Veal Loin with Summer Salad and Cucumber Coulis

Preheat the broiler. Peel, halve, and remove the pits from the peaches and nectarines, reserving the juices. Slice the peaches and nectarines into even slices. In a blender or food processor, puree half of the raspberries with 1 tablespoon of the sugar and a few drops of water until completely smooth. Strain through a fine sieve; set aside. Arrange the peach and nectarine slices in a decorative circle on 4 gratin dishes or in 4 wide-rim soup bowls.

Combine the egg yolks, the remaining 1 tablespoon of sugar, and white wine in a heatproof mixing bowl and, with the bowl immersed in boiling water or over low heat, whip vigorously until thick and foamy.

Spoon the egg yolk mixture over the fruits, covering them lightly. Place the dishes under the preheated broiler for 1 to 2 minutes, or until the glaze begins to bubble and lightly brown.

Garnish the gratins with the remaining 1 cup of raspberries. Spoon a small amount of raspberry puree on each dish, and dust the gratins lightly with powdered sugar. Serve immediately.

Hot Figs and Apricots
with Mirabelle Plum Ice Cream

Serves 4

Figs, apricots, and plums are summer's special treats, and in combination they are simply out of this world. The technique of cooking fresh fruit very lightly in caramelized sugar and serving it hot over ice cream can be used for many fruits. Be sure not to overcook the fruits. Crisp cookies make a great accompaniment.

8 to 12 fresh figs (Black Mission, Calamyrna, Kadota, or
*   Adriatica), or an equal amount of dried figs and 2*
*   tablespoons red wine or port*
4 ripe apricots, or 4 dried apricots and ¼ cup dry white wine
3 tablespoons butter
2 tablespoons sugar
1 tablespoon heavy cream
½ lemon (optional)

1 pint Plum Ice Cream, page 179, made with mirabelles, or
*   any good-quality plum, blackberry, cherry, or raspberry*
*   ice cream*

Wash the fresh figs and slice in half lengthwise. If using dried figs, soak them in the red wine or port for 30 minutes; set aside in the soaking liquid. Pit the apricots by cutting them in half lengthwise. If using dried apricots, soak them in the white wine for 30 minutes, then drain.

Heat a medium-sized non-aluminum skillet over medium heat. Add 1 tablespoon of the butter and, when it begins to foam, add the figs and apricots. Toss lightly with 1 teaspoon of the sugar for 1 minute, or until barely heated. Remove the fruit from the skillet and keep warm. Add the remaining sugar to the pan and, stirring constantly, cook the sugar until light amber brown. Add the remaining butter carefully (the mixture will foam), stirring continually. When incorporated, add the cream and stir until combined.

Return the fruit to the skillet and stir gently until coated. Adjust the sweetness with a light squeeze of lemon if necessary. Spoon the ice cream onto chilled plates and spoon the warm fruit compote around the ice cream. Serve immediately.

Peach and Nectarine Gratin with Raspberry Coulis

Blueberry Cobbler with Orange Custard

Serves 4 to 6

Cobblers are a universal favorite and a wonderful way to serve ripe summer berries. Much in vogue in the past few years, these easy-to-prepare desserts burst with the flavor of fruit and berries.

4 to 6 pints blueberries
1/3 cup sugar
Juice of 1 lemon
2 cups cake flour
1 teaspoon salt
1 tablespoon baking powder
1 cup sugar
8 tablespoons unsalted butter, chilled
3 large eggs, lightly beaten
3/4 cup milk
Sugar for sprinkling

ORANGE CUSTARD
1 cup heavy cream
1 tablespoon sugar
Grated zest and juice of 1 orange
4 eggs
1 teaspoon cornstarch dissolved in 1 teaspoon water

GARNISH
1 orange
4 mint sprigs

Preheat the oven to 350°. Wash and clean the blueberries well. In a large bowl, toss the berries with the sugar and the lemon juice. Pour the berries into a lightly buttered 2½-quart baking dish.

In a large bowl, sift together the flour, salt, baking powder, and sugar. Cut the butter into small pieces and, working either with your hands, a pastry cutter, or 2 knives, blend the butter into the flour mixture until it resembles coarse cornmeal. Combine the eggs with the milk and gently stir into the flour to make a moist dough; do not overmix.

With a mixing spoon or a plastic scraper, slowly spread the batter over the fruit with a sweeping motion, allowing the batter to fall off in a ribbon, and leaving a 1-inch strip of the berries uncovered around the rim; do not spread or smooth the batter. Sprinkle the top of the batter lightly with sugar. Bake for 45 minutes in the preheated oven, or until a tester inserted in the center of the dough comes out clean.

While the cobbler is baking, prepare the custard. In a small saucepan heat the cream and sugar. Add the orange zest and juice to the cream. Whip the eggs in a small bowl until combined and whip in half of the hot cream. Slowly whip the egg mixture into the cream mixture in the saucepan, along with the cornstarch mixture. Whisk continuously until the cream begins to thicken. Immediately remove from heat and pour into a serving container or bowl. Keep warm, whisking occasionally. Peel and segment the orange for garnish, adding any juice to the custard.

Remove the cobbler from the oven and let it cool for 10 minutes. Carefully spoon through the crust, serving a generous amount of berries and crust per person. Spoon the warm orange custard carefully over one corner of each serving, and garnish with orange segments and mint sprigs. Serve warm.

Blueberry Cobbler with Orange Custard

Peach Crisp with Blackberry Sauce

Serves 4 to 6

One of the highlights of summer in the Northwest is a juicy, ripe peach in hand with more within reach. Washington peaches are superb, and this crisp, with its tangy blackberry sauce, is pure perfection.

8 to 10 ripe peaches
¼ cup sugar
2 teaspoons freshly grated lemon zest
1 teaspoon cornstarch
Juice of 1 lemon

TOPPING
2½ cups unbleached all-purpose flour
¼ cup brown sugar
¼ cup granulated sugar
½ teaspoon salt
6 tablespoons butter, chilled
Granulated sugar for sprinkling

BLACKBERRY SAUCE
1 pint blackberries
2 tablespoons crème de cassis
2 tablespoons sugar
1 teaspoon fresh lemon juice

Whipped cream, crème fraîche, or ice cream

Preheat the oven to 375°. Peel the peaches by dropping them into boiling water for 5 seconds, then immersing them in ice water. Remove the peel, cut the peaches in half, and remove the pits. Cut each half into 6 sections and combine with the sugar in a large bowl. Add the lemon zest. Dissolve the cornstarch in the lemon juice and add to the peach mixture. Pour into a lightly buttered 2½-quart baking dish.

To make the topping   In a large bowl, combine the flour, brown sugar, granulated sugar, and salt. With your hands, a pastry cutter, or 2 knives, blend the butter into the mixture carefully until it resembles coarse cornmeal. Do not overwork; the topping should remain powdery. Sprinkle the topping over the peaches. You should have enough to cover the peaches completely to a depth of ¼ to ½ inch. Sprinkle the topping lightly with granulated sugar. Bake in the preheated oven for 35 to 45 minutes, or until the topping is evenly browned and the filling is bubbling lightly.

While the crisp is baking, prepare the sauce. Reserve several attractive blackberries for garnish. Puree the remainder in a blender or food processor with the cassis and sugar. Taste for sweetness and add lemon juice as necessary. Strain to remove all seeds.

Allow the crisp to rest for 10 minutes after removing from the oven. Carefully spoon some crisp onto each plate, being careful that the topping remains intact on each serving. Spoon the blackberry sauce around each serving of crisp and garnish the plates with fresh peach slices and clusters of the blackberries. Serve warm with whipped cream, crème fraîche, or ice cream.

Summer Preserves

Here is a delightful alchemy: the essence of summer distilled to liquid gold and sealed in a jar. This recipe is for refrigerated preserves, which use a minimum of sugar and have a more natural fruit taste; they also freeze beautifully.

Nectarine-Peach Preserves

Makes 2 quarts

8 cups sliced peeled nectarines or peaches (about 4 pounds)
5 cups sugar
⅓ cup fresh lemon juice

Slice the fruit, reserving all the juice, and place in a large non-aluminum bowl. Carefully mix in the sugar and lemon juice. Let sit at room temperature for 3 to 5 hours.

Place the mixture in a heavy non-aluminum saucepan and cook over low heat until the fruit is translucent, about 25 minutes. Remove the fruit with a slotted spoon. Simmer the syrup over low heat until reduced by half, about 25 minutes, stirring occasionally. Add the fruit to the syrup; return to a simmer and pack into jars.

These preserves will keep indefinitely in covered jars in the refrigerator and can be frozen with excellent results.

Plum Preserves

Makes 2 quarts

8 cups sliced unpeeled greengage, Italian, Damson,
*   mirabelle, or other firm, ripe plums (about 4 pounds)*
6 cups sugar

Prepare the plums in the sugar as described in the main recipe; and allow to macerate for 12 hours.

Place the fruit in a heavy, non-aluminum pot and simmer over as low a heat as possible for about 1 hour and 15 minutes. Remove the fruit from the syrup and cook barely at a simmer until the syrup is reduced by half. Combine with the fruit and store as described above.

Note   Cherries may also be prepared using this method.

Blueberry Preserves

Makes 2 quarts

8 cups blueberries
4 cups sugar
⅓ cup fresh lemon juice

Follow the main recipe, macerating the berries for 45 minutes and cooking them for about 5 minutes before removing the fruit and reducing the syrup.

Note   Raspberries and gooseberries may also be prepared using this method.

AUTUMN

AUTUMN

Summer's passing is often slow in the Northwest. The moist fragrance of forest and field rises cool in the damp morning air and warms in the sun-filled days. For the cook, the changing season speaks a special language: the sweet tang of cider, the scent of apples, alder smoke, pungent mushrooms, roasting nuts. And the chill nights bring the warmth of hearty soups and stews filled with the tastes of summer. Kettles of vibrant-colored jams and jellies are prepared to fill jars for winter, and the fruits, vegetables, game, and seafood of autumn seem all the more wonderful with each fleeting day.

One of the greatest pleasures of the Pacific Northwest is its array of large and small game: deer, elk, moose, bear, ducks, geese, pheasant, grouse, and quail. Game cookery is a world all its own, and cooler nights remind us of the succulent meats of autumn days afield.

Autumn brings new excitement and inspiration to the kitchen. Peaches and nectarines are replaced by the juicy nectar of Anjou, Comice, Bosc, and Bartlett pears. With crimson and fire-yellow leaves comes the sweetness of Damson, Italian, mirabelle and greengage plums. But these are just an overture to the arrival of the simplest and finest fruit of all: apples in their countless varieties and tastes. How can one possibly be the favorite? Gravenstein, Rome, Gala, Criterion, Northern Spy, Jonathan, Jonagold, Winesap, McIntosh, and countless more—each as delicious as the next.

Before the first frost, the richness of the Northwest garden reaches its peak with corn, beans, and squash; crisp salad greens; tomatoes holding the last warmth of summer. Each taste seems more wonderful, as we feel the seasons slowly turning. The ancient tribes—Makah, Salish, Nez Percé—ritualized these days with symbols of fertile earth and seas, and we too are linked to that inner world as the earth's mysteries become manifest in the autumn harvest.

Fires warm the hearth once again, and the aroma of muffins, breads, fragrant cakes, and stuffings fills the kitchen. There are leaves blown across the garden path, apples fallen at the base of a gnarled tree trunk, pumpkins and cabbages piled high in weathered bins. The richness of field, sea, and forest is ours. The gift of the Northwest is here before us in both the minuscule and the majestic, and the fruits of the forest floors, rivers, bays, and mountains become the rich bounty of our table.

There are fragrant cèpes and chanterelles on the kitchen counter, the winy aroma of pears, and the spicy sweetness of stewing pumpkin. And someone is walking down the hill from the orchard, through the fading twilight and wood smoke, carrying an overflowing bushel basket.

Autumn Recipes

Hot Hazelnut Tarts with Oregon Blue Cheese

Oregon Cheddar Soup with Swiss Chard and Walnuts

Corn Chowder with Clam Fritters

Smoked Pheasant with Arugula, Artichokes, and Honey-Pepper Vinaigrette

Smoked Duck Breast with Wild Rice Salad, Pumpkin Chutney, and Ginger Vinaigrette

Autumn Mushroom Sampler

Wild Mushroom and Fig Brochettes with Watercress and Cranberries

Petrale Sole with Cèpes and Cider Butter Sauce

Steamed Wild Duck with Chanterelles

Roast Chukar Partridge with Rhubarb

Roast Pheasant with Cabbage, Quince, and Blackberry Honey

Roast Quail with Finn Potato Pancakes and Persimmons

Rack of Lamb with Hubbard Squash and Red Grapes

Roast Saddle of Venison with Chestnuts and Gooseberry-Cabernet Sauce

Baked Apples with Fireweed Honey and Cranberries

Apple Dumplings

Spiced Figs in Port with Anjou Pear Ice Cream

Shortbread Nut Cookies

Hazelnut Praline Torte with Espresso Cream

Five-Nut Torte

Hot Hazelnut Tarts
with Oregon Blue Cheese

Makes six 4-inch tart shells or one 10-inch shell

Oregon Blue is a buttery, rich, robust cheese made by the Rogue River Valley Creamery in Central Point, Oregon. It is wonderful to cook with, as it melts beautifully and retains all its flavor. Paired with Oregon hazelnuts, luscious onions, and a crackling-light pastry, it makes a scintillating appetizer. If you have some dough left, roll it out, cut it in strips, and sprinkle it with more cheese. Twist and bake at 350° until crisp to make delicious cheese sticks to serve with cocktails.

1¼ cups hazelnuts

PASTRY
1½ cups unbleached all-purpose flour
¼ teaspoon salt
¾ cup reserved skinned hazelnuts
10 tablespoons chilled butter, cut into small cubes
2 eggs, beaten
2 tablespoons ice water

FILLING
2 yellow, Vidalia, Walla Walla, or red onions
1 tablespoon butter
Salt and pepper to taste
3 eggs
⅔ cup heavy cream
½ teaspoon Dijon mustard

6 to 8 ounces Oregon Blue, Maytag, Roquefort, or Gorgonzola cheese for 4-inch tarts, or 1¼ pounds cheese for a 10-inch tart

TOPPING
½ cup reserved skinned hazelnuts
⅓ cup fine dry bread crumbs
1 tablespoon minced fresh chives
1 teaspoon minced fresh summer savory, oregano, or thyme
1 tablespoon clarified butter, page 165

Preheat the oven to 350°. Place the hazelnuts in an ovenproof skillet and toast in the preheated oven for 6 to 8 minutes. Let cool, then rub the skins off in a towel or with the palms of your hands.

To prepare the pastry   Sift the flour and salt into a large bowl. Grind the ¾ cup skinned hazelnuts in a blender, food processor, or nut grinder and add to the flour and salt. With your fingers, a pastry cutter, or 2 knives, cut the cold butter into the dry mixture until the mixture resembles oatmeal. Add the beaten eggs and the ice water and form into a ball, adding additional small amounts of water if necessary; do not overmix. Chill the dough.

To make the filling   Peel and julienne the onions. In a large skillet, melt the butter and add the onions; season with salt and pepper. Cover and cook for about 20 to 30 minutes, stirring occasionally, until the onions are lightly caramelized; set aside. In a medium bowl, whip the eggs, cream, and mustard together. Season with salt and pepper; set aside.

Preheat the oven to 375°. Roll the pastry dough ⅛ inch thick on a floured surface. Butter six 4-inch tart molds with removable

Hot Hazelnut Tarts with Oregon Blue Cheese and Walla Walla Onions

bottoms (or one 10-inch tart pan) and line with the dough, being careful not to tear or puncture the dough. Trim the dough and crimp the edges. When all the shells are completed, place a round sheet of aluminum foil in each shell and fill with dried beans, rice, or pie weights. Bake in the preheated oven for 8 to 10 minutes, or until lightly browned.

Reduce the oven temperature to 350°. Remove the shells from the oven and fill each with one fourth of the crumbled blue cheese and caramelized onions (they should be about two-thirds full). Pour the egg mixture over, being careful not to let it overflow. Return the shells to the oven on a baking sheet and bake at 350° for 15 to 25 minutes, or until set and lightly browned; remove from the oven.

Preheat the broiler or raise the oven temperature to 450°.

To make the topping   Grind the ½ cup skinned hazelnuts in a food processor, blender, or nut grinder. Combine the ground hazelnuts, bread crumbs, and minced herbs. Sprinkle over the top of the tarts. Drizzle the topping with butter and return to the oven or place under the broiler for 5 minutes, or until the topping is golden brown. If using a 10-inch shell, let it cool for 5 minutes, then slice into wedges. Serve immediately.

Oregon Cheddar Soup
with Swiss Chard and Walnuts

Serves 4

The best of the Oregon Cheddars—Tillamook Extra Sharp, Rogue River Gold, and Bandon—are rich, crumbly, smooth, and full of flavor. Serve this soup any time there's a chill in the air.

1 pound sharp Oregon, Vermont, New York State,
*   Wisconsin, or English Cheddar*
½ cup heavy cream
2 cups half and half
1½ teaspoons Worcestershire sauce
3 to 4 drops Tabasco sauce, or to taste
1 cup Chicken Stock, page 158, or canned chicken broth
Salt to taste
Juice of ½ lemon
Scant ⅛ teaspoon ground nutmeg
1 teaspoon butter
⅓ cup walnut halves
1 cup finely shredded Swiss chard or spinach leaves

Chop or grate the cheese coarsely. Place in the top of a double boiler with the cream, half and half, Worcestershire, and Tabasco. Keep the water in the double boiler slowly simmering, and stir the soup occasionally until it is completely smooth. Strain through a fine sieve if necessary. Add chicken stock if necessary to adjust consistency. Add the salt, lemon juice, and nutmeg.

Melt the butter in a heavy skillet and toast the walnuts over low heat. Drain on paper towels and keep warm.

Divide two thirds of the shredded Swiss chard among 4 heated bowls and ladle the soup over it. Garnish the top of the soup with the remaining Swiss chard and the toasted walnuts and serve at once.

Corn Chowder with Clam Fritters

Serves 4

Loads of sweet corn begin arriving in Northwest markets in early fall. This hearty corn chowder is a perfect blend of summer and autumn. The crisp clam fritters add a delicious contrast.

2 shallots, minced
2 garlic cloves, minced
1 teaspoon minced fresh parsley
½ teaspoon minced fresh thyme
¼ cup diced bacon
2 tablespoons butter
½ carrot, diced
½ medium onion, diced
1 celery stalk, diced
2½ to 3 cups Chicken Stock, page 158, or canned chicken broth
1 tablespoon Beurre Manie, page 165
1 cup heavy cream
2 ears corn
Salt and pepper to taste

CLAM FRITTERS
1 pound Manila clams in the shell
¼ cup dry white wine
Salt and pepper to taste
¼ cup unbleached all-purpose flour
2 egg yolks, beaten
1 tablespoon heavy cream
2 teaspoons ice water
¼ cup vegetable oil
1 teaspoon minced fresh chives
1 teaspoon minced fresh tarragon

In a large, heavy saucepan, sauté the shallots, garlic, and herbs with the bacon and 1 tablespoon of the butter over low heat for 10 minutes, or until softened and aromatic. Add the carrot, onion, and celery and sauté over low heat for 1 minute. Add the chicken stock, bring to a boil over high heat, and whip in the *beurre manie* in small pieces. Simmer 5 minutes, whisking occasionally. Add the cream and bring to a boil. Shuck the corn and scrape the kernels off the cobs with a sharp knife. Add to the chowder, stirring well, and adjust the seasoning; keep warm.

To make the fritters   Scrub the clams and steam them in the white wine just until opened. Strain the liquid into the chowder and shell the clams into a small bowl; season lightly. Toss the clams with 1 tablespoon of the flour. Combine the egg yolks with the remaining flour, cream, and ice water and dip the clams in the batter. Heat the oil in a heavy skillet. Drop the clams into the hot oil and fry until browned and crisp. Remove from the pan with a slotted spoon and drain on paper towels.

Ladle the hot chowder into 4 wide-rim soup bowls and garnish with the fritters and the minced herbs. Serve immediately.

Note   This soup is also delicious prepared with smoked pheasant stock (see page 158) and garnished with smoked pheasant meat cut into julienne instead of the clam fritters.

Corn Chowder with Clam Fritters

Smoked Pheasant with Arugula, Artichokes, and Honey-Pepper Vinaigrette

Serves 4

One 2½-pound pheasant, 2 boneless pheasant breasts, 4
quail, or 2 double chicken breasts
12 baby artichokes, or 4 medium artichokes
2 quarts water mixed with 2 tablespoons salt
1 lemon, cut in half
Basic Vinaigrette, page 165
2 teaspoons honey
½ teaspoon black peppercorns, crushed
2 bunches arugula

Bone and skin the breasts of the whole pheasant as described on page 149, reserving the legs for stew or pâté (or your butcher can do this for you easily). Or you may want to brine the whole bird, using the smoked legs and thighs for Corn Chowder, page 77.

Cure and smoke the pheasant breasts as described on page 152. Cool to room temperature and refrigerate for several hours or overnight.

To prepare the artichokes   If using small artichokes, simply boil them in the salted water until the inner leaves can be removed easily with the fingertips, about 15 to 20 minutes. Drain and cool immediately in ice water to prevent further cooking. Trim the very tip of the artichoke, a few of the outer leaves, and the stem. Cut in half lengthwise and rub with the cut lemon. If using large artichokes, follow the same procedure and, when they are completely chilled, trim off the tough outer leaves and the base of the stem. Save some of the leaves for garnish. Cut 1 inch to 1½ inches off the tip of the artichoke, split the artichoke in

half lengthwise, and remove the choke. Quarter the artichoke, rub it with the cut lemon, and set aside.

Prepare the vinaigrette; add the honey and the crushed peppercorns. Remove any large stems from the arugula; wash it and dry it well. In a small bowl, toss the arugula with 1 tablespoon of the vinaigrette, or just enough to coat the leaves. Arrange the arugula in the center of the plate, along with the artichokes.

Slice the smoked pheasant breasts on the bias into ¼-inch-thick slices. Spoon a small amount of the vinaigrette onto the plates and fan the slices decoratively over the top.

Smoked Duck Breast with Wild Rice Salad, Pumpkin Chutney, and Ginger Vinaigrette

Serves 4

This flavorful autumn salad is highlighted by a spicy vinaigrette. Squab, pheasant, quail, or any game bird works beautifully in this dish.

One 2½- to 3½-pound duck, boned, or 2 duck breasts

WILD RICE SALAD
1 tablespoon peanut oil
2 shallots, minced
¼ cup diced celery
¼ cup diced carrot

3 tablespoons minced Methow Valley, Virginia, Missouri, or
   any good-quality smoked ham
½ cup wild rice
2½ cups Chicken Stock, page 158, or canned chicken broth
Salt and pepper to taste
Basic Vinaigrette, page 165
½ teaspoon minced fresh ginger

PUMPKIN CHUTNEY
½ cup dry white wine
¾ cup cider vinegar
¼ cup water
3 tablespoons brown sugar
¼ teaspoon ground cinnamon
Pinch ground nutmeg
¼ cup raisins
1 pound fresh pumpkin, peeled, seeded, and cut into large
   dice (about 1 cup)
⅓ cup walnuts
¼ teaspoon minced fresh sage

Chicory or curly leaf lettuce
4 thyme or sage sprigs

If using a whole duck, bone the duck as described on page 149. Brine and smoke the duck breasts according to the directions on page 152. Preheat the oven to 350°. (Reserve the legs and thighs for pâté, or brine and smoke the legs to use as a soup garnish, or with pasta or risotto.) Heat the oil in a skillet and lightly sauté the shallots, celery, carrot, and ham for 2 minutes; set aside.

Place the wild rice in a shallow 2- to 3-quart baking dish. Pour 2½ cups of the chicken stock over the rice and season with salt and pepper. Cover and bake for 25 to 35 minutes, or until the rice is tender and fluffy, adding up to ½ cup more chicken stock if necessary. Let cool to room temperature. Prepare the vinaigrette. Add the minced ginger, stirring well. Let sit for 10 minutes.

To make the chutney In a non-aluminum saucepan, bring the white wine, vinegar, water, sugar, and spices to a boil. Add the raisins and simmer for 10 minutes. Add the diced pumpkin, simmer for 2 minutes, remove from the heat, and cover loosely. Allow to cool to room temperature, add the walnuts and sage, and refrigerate for 2 hours or overnight.

Remove the skin from the smoked duck breasts. Slice the breasts thinly on the bias. Add the vegetable-ham mixture to the wild rice, along with 2 to 3 tablespoons of the vinaigrette, and toss. Place some chicory leaves on each of the 4 chilled plates. Mound the wild rice salad onto the chicory. Lay the thin slices of duck breast around the rice. Spoon a small amount of the chutney on the side of the rice, and spoon the vinaigrette around the breast slices. Garnish with the thyme or sage sprigs, if desired.

Autumn Mushroom Sampler

Serves 4

Nothing can compare to the taste of this dish, prepared with a few of the many kinds of edible mushrooms that abound in autumn in the Pacific Northwest. Many other mushrooms can be substituted and the proportions changed. Their cooking times will vary, but can be easily determined by their size and texture.

2 cups (8 medium) chanterelles
1 cup (10 to 12 small) cèpes or boletes
1 to 2 cups (4 medium) matsutakes
1 cup hen of the woods mushrooms
2 ounces lobster mushrooms
2 to 4 medium shiitakes
1 tablespoon clarified butter, page 165
Salt and fresh ground pepper to taste
3 tablespoons Marsala or cognac
1 teaspoon veal, chicken, or mushroom essence, page 163
   (optional)
2 tablespoons butter

Trim all the mushrooms to about the same size. Clean the mushrooms well with a vegetable brush or damp kitchen towel. In a medium-sized heavy skillet, heat the clarified butter until it begins to smoke. Add all the mushrooms except the cèpes and hen of the woods. Season lightly. Toss the mushrooms until they are lightly browned; lower the heat to medium until the mushrooms exude their liquid. Raise the heat to high and add the Marsala or cognac and the remaining mushrooms; reduce to a glaze. Remove from the heat. Add the essence, along with

a few drops of water, until the mixture is blended. Return to the heat and whisk in the butter; do not boil. Adjust the seasoning and serve immediately.

Wild Mushroom and Fig Brochettes
with Watercress and Cranberries

Serves 4

This colorful dish offers a pleasant blend of flavors and textures. It may be prepared with almost any wild mushroom. Be careful to grill the brochettes lightly just before serving.

8 ounces morels, shiitakes, chanterelles, cèpes, or oyster
   mushrooms
12 fresh or dried Black Mission, Calamyrna, or Kadota figs,
   halved (if using dried, soak for 1 hour in red wine)
⅔ cup cranberries
Basic Vinaigrette, page 165
8 to 12 chives
1 tarragon sprig
1 thyme sprig
2 garlic cloves, crushed
2 tablespoons sugar
3 bunches watercress

Prepare a wood or charcoal fire in an open grill and allow to burn down to white-red coals. Preheat the oven to 350°. Prepare four brochettes by alternately threading the mushrooms and figs tightly on bamboo skewers. If desired, a few raw cranberries can be skewered in the middle of each brochette.

Prepare the vinaigrette; add the herbs and garlic to ¼ cup of the vinaigrette. Place the brochettes in a non-aluminum container and toss with the herbed vinaigrette. Marinate for 10 minutes.

Toss the cranberries with the sugar and place on a baking sheet. Bake in the preheated oven for 5 to 8 minutes. The cranberries must remain firm and the sugar melt. Cool the cranberries to room temperature.

Preheat the broiler, if using. Wash the watercress, drain, and dry. Place the brochettes on the hot grill for 2 minutes on one side, or under the broiler for 3 to 4 minutes. Turn the brochettes and cook for 1 more minute; remove from the heat.

Toss the watercress in a small amount of the remaining vinaigrette, add two thirds of the cranberries, and divide the salad among 4 room-temperature plates. Place a brochette on top of the watercress on each plate, remove the skewers, and sprinkle a few of the reserved cranberries around the salad. Serve immediately.

Wild Mushroom and Fig Brochettes with Watercress and Cranberries

Petrale Sole with Cèpes and Cider Butter Sauce

Serves 4

Petrale sole is one of the most underrated of North American fish. It is sweet and flavorful and sautés beautifully. Paired with the richness of cèpes and the smoothness of Cider Butter Sauce, it is a subtle, elegant dish. Acorn, Hubbard, or Danish squash sautéed with apples and the nicest green vegetable available make a delicious accompaniment.

CIDER BUTTER SAUCE
1 teaspoon peanut oil
1 shallot, chopped
4 mushrooms, chopped
1 thyme sprig
½ cup cider vinegar
½ unpeeled Jonathan or Winesap apple, cored and chopped
2 cups unfiltered apple cider
1 teaspoon heavy cream
4 to 6 tablespoons butter, cut into pieces

8 ounces cèpes
2 teaspoons peanut oil
1 tablespoon Marsala
2 tablespoons butter, cut in pieces
Salt and pepper to taste
2 tablespoons peanut oil
1½ pounds petrale sole

To prepare the sauce   In a heavy, medium-sized saucepan, heat the oil and sauté the shallot, mushrooms, and thyme until the shallot is translucent. Add the cider vinegar and the chopped apple and boil until the vinegar is almost evaporated. Add ¾ cup of the cider and boil rapidly until the cider is reduced to a glaze. Add another ¾ cup and repeat. Add the final ½ cup and reduce again. Whisk in the cream. Remove from the heat and whisk in the butter pieces. Strain through a fine sieve, pressing out all the liquid. Adjust the seasoning and keep warm.

Wash the cèpes and dry them well. Heat a heavy skillet over high heat, add the oil, and sauté the cèpes for 10 seconds. Add the Marsala, toss lightly, and reduce until nearly evaporated. Swirl the butter into the cèpes. Add the seasoning and keep warm.

In a medium-sized skillet over high heat, heat the oil and sauté 2 portions of the fish for 1 minute on the first side, then turn it over and remove it to a warm platter. Keep hot. Sauté the remaining sole; add seasoning and keep warm.

Divide the cèpes equally among 4 heated plates. Spoon a small amount of the sauce on each plate. Place the fish on each plate and serve immediately.

Steamed Wild Duck with Chanterelles

Serves 4

From the marshes of Washington's Skagit Valley and Grand Coulee Basin, and Oregon's Willamette and coastal valleys, comes another of autumn's greatest foods, wild duck. Teal, fantail, and mallard are all full flavored and rich. They are greatly

Petrale Sole with Cèpes and Cider Butter Sauce

enhanced by the techniques in this recipe—steaming and roasting—and the result offers crisp skin, flavorful meat, and a marvelous sauce made from the steaming liquid. The size, age, and tenderness of the ducks will vary the roasting and steaming times. The duck should be medium rare when served. Canadian goose is also delicious prepared this way. The cooking time will be closer to that of a domestic duck and, like wild duck, it is best served medium rare.

4 wild ducks, approximately 1½ pounds each, or 2 domestic
    ducks, 3 to 4 pounds each
Salt and pepper to taste
½ ounce dried orange peel (available in Asian markets)
1 ounce dried Asian mushrooms (available in Asian
    markets)
2 cups soy sauce or tamari
½ cup dry sherry or rice wine
1 tablespoon chopped fresh ginger
2 heads star anise
3 shallots, chopped
½ cup honey
2 thyme sprigs
1 medium tamarind pod, optional (available in Asian
    markets)
¼ cup chopped lotus root, optional (available in Asian
    markets)
3 garlic cloves, crushed
1 tablespoon peanut oil
8 ounces chanterelles
2 tablespoons Marsala
2 tablespoons butter, cut into pieces
1 teaspoon cornstarch dissolved in 1 teaspoon water

Wash the ducks inside and out and dry well. Season well with salt and pepper inside and out.

Soak the dried orange peel and the dried mushrooms in 3 tablespoons of the soy sauce or tamari mixed with 2 tablespoons of the sherry for 15 minutes. When reconstituted, combine with the ginger, star anise, and shallots. Stuff the cavity of each duck with this mixture.

Heat ½ cup of the soy sauce with the honey until warm and brush each duck well with this mixture. Repeat until the mixture is completely used and the ducks are well coated.

Preheat the oven to 475°. Set the ducks on a roasting rack in a roasting pan with a lid. Roast uncovered in the preheated oven for 10 minutes for wild ducks, 20 minutes for domestic, or until the skin is lightly browned and the fats are being rendered. Reduce the heat to 400° and continue roasting for approximately 5 minutes for wild ducks, 15 minutes for domestic.

Carefully remove the roasting pan from the oven. Discard all the fat. Combine the remaining soy sauce or tamari, the remaining sherry, the thyme, tamarind, lotus root, and garlic in the roaster. Place the pan over high heat. Bring the liquid to a boil, then reduce to a simmer. Cover tightly and steam for about 20 minutes. Baste the ducks several times with the liquid and return to the oven uncovered for 10 minutes for wild ducks, 25 minutes for domestic. To test the duck for doneness, test with meat thermometer at the thigh joint; it should read 140° for medium rare. Or make an incision with a knife at the thigh; the meat should be pink at the joint.

Meanwhile, in a medium skillet, heat the peanut oil and sauté the chanterelles for 2 minutes. Add salt and pepper to taste. Add the Marsala and boil until evaporated. Swirl in the butter pieces; keep warm.

Remove the ducks from the oven to a cutting board set over a tray to catch any juices. Bone the ducks as described on page 149, reserving all the juices and discarding the excess fat on the legs. Add the juices to the steaming liquid. Remove all the fat from the steaming liquid and whisk the cornstarch mixture into the liquid to thicken it. Slice the duck breasts and arrange on 4 hot plates with the legs. Spoon the chanterelles into the center of the plates. Ladle a small amount of the sauce onto each plate if desired. Serve immediately, accompanied by the sauce.

Steamed Wild Duck with Chanterelles

Roast Chukar Partridge with Rhubarb

Serves 4

The partridge, a distant cousin of the grouse, is an upland game bird whose habitat ranges from Northern California to Washington, Idaho, and Montana. It is full flavored and sublime and demands meticulous cooking. Pheasant or quail are also delicious prepared in this manner. Oven-roasted potatoes and lightly sautéed yellow squash are fine accompaniments.

¾ to 1 pound rhubarb, green stems removed
¼ cup sugar
2 tablespoons Cabernet Sauvignon wine, or any good-
*   quality dry red wine*
3 shallots, minced
1 teaspoon minced fresh ginger
⅓ cup raisins
Pinch each ground nutmeg, allspice, and cinnamon
1 thyme sprig, 1 teaspoon crushed peppercorns, 1 bay leaf,
*   and 3 to 4 whole cloves tied in a cheesecloth bag*

SAUCE
1 teaspoon peanut oil
2 shallots
2 garlic cloves
½ medium carrot
¼ medium onion
½ celery stalk
2 thyme sprigs
1 tarragon sprig
Game bird carcasses or bones, if available
2 quarts Game Stock, page 158, Chicken Stock, page 158, or
*   canned chicken broth*

4 chukars, blue grouse, ruffled grouse, or pheasant,
*   approximately 12 to 14 ounces each, preferably wild*
Salt and pepper to taste
2 tablespoons peanut oil

Peel and dice the rhubarb uniformly into ½-inch pieces. In a heavy saucepan, toss the rhubarb with the sugar until it is coated. Cook over low heat for 2 to 3 minutes, or until the sugar begins to melt, and add the wine, shallots, ginger, raisins, spices, and bag of herbs. Simmer, stirring occasionally and being careful not to break the rhubarb pieces, until the rhubarb is tender but retains its shape. Remove from the saucepan and set aside.

To make the sauce   In a heavy saucepan, heat the oil and sauté the shallots, garlic, vegetables, herbs, and any game bird trimmings until lightly browned. Add 1 cup of the stock and reduce over high heat to 1 tablespoon. Repeat the reduction process twice more and add the remaining stock. Simmer for 25 minutes, carefully skimming any impurities, until the sauce lightly coats a spoon. Strain through a fine sieve, pressing out all the liquids. Keep warm.

Preheat the oven to 475°. Season the birds well with salt and pepper, including the body cavities. Heat the 2 tablespoons oil in a heavy skillet or roasting pan and brown the birds well on all sides. Turn breast-side down and roast in the preheated oven for 8 to 10 minutes. Lower the heat to 200°. Remove the birds from the oven, place on a heatproof platter, and return them to the oven for approximately 10 minutes. Place the roasting pan on high heat and add ½ cup of the sauce, scraping any browned bits off the bottom of the pan. Strain into the remaining sauce. Disjoint the birds as described on page 149, adding all the juices to the sauce. Season the sauce to taste.

Slice the breasts on the bias and fan out over 4 heated plates. Place a leg and thigh behind the breast slices and spoon the rhubarb into the center. Ladle the sauce around the partridge and serve at once.

Roast Pheasant with Cabbage, Quince, and Blackberry Honey

Serves 4

Wild pheasants, properly handled, have a taste that pen-raised birds can never duplicate. Birds should be well dressed, rinsed, and refrigerated for 2 to 3 days with feathers on. Wild pheasants must also be very carefully cooked, as they can overcook in a minute and be very disappointing. Here is a fine method for cooking pheasant or any game bird.

4 wild pheasants, or 2 farm-raised pheasants
Salt and pepper to taste
½ head red cabbage, cored and finely shredded (about 2
*   cups)*
½ head Savoy cabbage, cored and finely shredded (about 2
*   cups)*
½ cup dry red wine
2 tablespoons red wine vinegar
1 quince, peeled and cut into medium dice

SAUCE
2 teaspoons butter
½ medium onion, chopped
1 carrot, chopped
1 celery stalk, chopped
3 shallots, chopped
1 thyme sprig
1 teaspoon black peppercorns, crushed
¼ cup blackberry honey or any good-quality honey
1 tablespoon red wine vinegar
1 to 1½ quarts Game Stock (made with pheasants), page
*   158, Chicken Stock, page 158, or canned chicken broth*

1 tablespoon peanut oil

Preheat the oven to 450°. Season the pheasants with salt and pepper on the outside and inside. Set aside at room temperature. Combine the cabbage with the red wine, vinegar, and quince in a non-aluminum pan and cook over low heat, covered, for 10 to 15 minutes, stirring occasionally; set aside.

To prepare the sauce   In a heavy saucepan, melt the butter and sauté the vegetables, thyme, and black peppercorns over medium heat (along with any available game bird bones or trimmings) until lightly browned. Add the honey and, stirring constantly, cook until it is aromatic and begins to caramelize. Add the vinegar and continue to stir constantly until evaporated. Add 1 cup of the pheasant stock and reduce to 1 to 2 tablespoons. Add 1 cup stock twice more, reducing it to a thick syrup each time. Add the remaining stock, turn the heat to low, and simmer the sauce, carefully skimming off any impurities, until it is clear and begins to coat a spoon; strain, set aside, and keep warm.

Over medium-high heat, heat a heavy skillet large enough to hold all the birds. The birds can also be browned individually and placed in a roaster, but it is preferable to brown them and roast them in the same pan. Brown the birds evenly in the peanut oil and, turning them breast-side down in the pan, roast them in the oven for 8 to 10 minutes. Remove from the oven immediately, reduce the heat to 200°, and leave the oven door open. Remove the birds from the roasting pan and transfer them to an ovenproof dish or baking pan to hold their juices. When the oven cools to 200°, return the birds to the oven for about 25 to 35 minutes. Test for doneness by lightly scoring the skin between the leg and breast and opening the leg enough to allow you to check the joint; the flesh should still be pinkish-red. If using larger, domestic pheasants, increase the initial cooking time by 10 minutes, and allow to sit at 200° for an additional 20 minutes.

Meanwhile, pour off the fat from the roasting pan. Add 2 tablespoons of the sauce, scraping up any browned bits from the

pan, and reduce to a glaze. Strain into the remaining sauce. Disjoint the pheasant by first slicing through the skin between the thigh and breast until you reach the joint. Holding the drumstick, open the leg and cut through the joint to separate the leg. Repeat with the other leg, and separate the thigh from the drumstick with the heel of the knife.

With the neck cavity facing away from you, run the knife along the breastbone the length of the breast. Turn the breast so the neck faces you, run the knife along the wishbone, and, guiding your knife along the rib cage, remove the breast from the bone. Repeat on the other breast. The breast should still be underdone. Return the portioned pieces to the 200° oven until they reach the desired doneness. Reserve all the bones and juices for stock. The bones may also be chopped into small pieces, browned in a pan on top of the stove, and added to the simmering stock before straining.

Allow the stock to simmer an additional 30 minutes. Hold the pheasants at room temperature at this stage and, when ready to serve, return the portioned pieces to the roasting pan and place in the oven, still set at 200°, for approximately 10 minutes. When ready to serve, strain the sauce through a fine sieve, pressing out all the liquids; keep warm.

Slice the breasts on the bias and arrange on 4 heated plates, placing a thigh and leg behind each breast. Adjust the seasoning of the braised cabbage and quince and spoon onto the center of the plate behind the breast. Reheat the sauce and adjust the seasoning. Ladle the sauce around the plate and serve immediately.

Roast Quail with Finn Potato Pancakes and Persimmons

Serves 4

The wheatlands of Eastern Oregon and Washington are a bird hunter's paradise, and tender quail is one of the many fine game birds available this time of year. Be sure not to overcook them; they should be still pink at the joints. This recipe is also very good with pheasant, grouse, or duck. The pancakes, served with applesauce or fruit preserves, are fantastic for brunch or breakfast. Finn potatoes, sweet yellow-fleshed early-crop potatoes from the Skagit Valley, are especially good roasted or fried.

Quail Natural Juice, page 159
12 ounces Finn or russet potatoes
12 ounces yellow onions
2 eggs
Salt and white pepper to taste
3 to 4 ripe persimmons
4 tablespoons clarified butter, page 165
6 tablespoons peanut oil
12 quail

Prepare the Quail Sauce; set aside and keep warm.

Preheat the oven to 450°. Peel the potatoes and set them aside in water. Peel the onions. Grate the potatoes on a hand grater or in a food processor into 1½-inch-long pieces. Grate the onions on the same-sized attachment and combine with the potatoes.

Roast Pheasant with Cabbage, Quince, and Blackberry Honey

Beat the eggs and add to the potato-onion mixture. Season with salt and pepper and set aside. Peel the persimmons and slice into 12 even slices; set aside.

Heat a small, heavy skillet over medium heat and add 2 tablespoons of the clarified butter and 2 tablespoons of the peanut oil. Spoon out 3 tablespoons of the potato-onion mixture and carefully drop into the hot fat, gently flattening the mound with the spoon. Repeat until the skillet is full. Sauté until golden brown and crisp on each side and remove from the skillet to a platter lined with paper towels. Transfer to a baking sheet and keep warm. Repeat the procedure until half the batter has been cooked.

Heat a large skillet over high heat and add 2 tablespoons of the peanut oil. Salt and pepper the quails inside and out and sauté them until evenly browned.

Transfer the skillet to the preheated oven and roast the quails for 5 to 10 minutes, or until they are pink at the joints. Remove from the oven, lower the heat to 250°, transfer the quails to a heated platter to keep warm.

While the quails are roasting, heat the remaining 2 tablespoons butter and 2 tablespoons oil in the small skillet and prepare the remainder of the potato pancakes, draining them on paper towels and then adding them to the baking sheet.

Disjoint the quail at each leg and remove each breast as described on page 149. Place the pancakes in the oven for 5 minutes to crisp, then divide them equally among 4 heated plates. Surround the pancakes with the persimmon slices and arrange the quail on top, allowing 3 quail per person, or 2 if large. Bring the sauce to a boil and ladle around the quail. Serve immediately.

Rack of Lamb with Hubbard Squash and Red Grapes

Serves 4

The lamb of eastern Washington, especially the area around Ellensburg, is some of the finest in the world. The pastureland is rich and lush, and the lamb matures to a full-flavored peak. The most easily digestible of red meats, lamb is high in protein and, if cooked correctly, low in fat. This dish includes the richness of squash and the sweetness of red grapes.

4 lamb racks (4 bones per rack)
2 tablespoons minced fresh parsley
2 tablespoons minced fresh tarragon

¼ cup finely ground fresh bread crumbs
2 tablespoons peanut oil
1 tablespoon whole-grain mustard
2 shallots, minced
*1 pound Hubbard, acorn, or butternut squash, peeled,
    seeded, and cut into large dice (1½ to 2 cups)*
Salt and pepper to taste
½ cup Chicken Stock, page 158, or canned chicken broth
2 tablespoons Marsala
Lamb Natural Juice, page 159
1 tablespoon butter
¾ cup seedless red or green grapes

Preheat the oven to 400°. Prepare the racks by removing all fat and scraping the bones clean, or have your butcher prepare them for you. Allow them to rest at room temperature while you prepare the herb mixture. Add the parsley and tarragon to

Roast Quail with Finn Potato Pancakes and Persimmons

the bread crumbs. In a heavy skillet, sauté the racks over high heat in 1 tablespoon of the peanut oil until evenly browned; remove. Brush the racks very lightly with the mustard and dip each into the herb mixture, pressing the crumbs lightly onto the lamb. Return to the oven and roast to the desired doneness, about 10 to 12 minutes for medium rare.

In a skillet, sauté the shallots over low heat for 2 minutes in the remaining 1 tablespoon peanut oil and add the squash, tossing lightly. Raise the heat to high, season the mixture with salt and pepper, and add the stock. Lower the heat and simmer un-til the stock is reduced and the squash is crisp-tender, about 5 minutes. Remove from the heat and keep warm. Remove the racks from the oven and allow to rest for 5 minutes.

Add the Marsala to the roasting pan and reduce to a glaze, scraping up any browned bits. Add the lamb natural juice and bring to a boil; strain. Return to a boil, swirl in the butter, and add the grapes, heating them just enough to warm them through. Slice the racks into 4 bone-in slices per person and divide among 4 preheated plates. Spoon the squash onto each plate, spoon the sauce around the racks, and serve immediately.

Roast Saddle of Venison with Chestnuts and Gooseberry-Cabernet Sauce

Serves 4

This classically inspired venison dish is at its best with fresh gooseberries, but it is also delicious with preserved gooseberries. Oven-roasted potatoes and Brussels sprouts or baked acorn squash are excellent accompaniments.

2 tablespoons peanut oil
2 shallots, chopped
6 medium mushrooms, chopped
½ teaspoon black peppercorns, crushed
1 bay leaf
2 thyme sprigs
2 cups Cabernet Sauvignon wine, or any good-quality dry red wine
4 to 6 cups Venison Stock, page 159, Veal Stock, page 157, or canned low-salt beef broth

24 chestnuts (about 1 pound)
1 cup fresh or preserved gooseberries, page 67
1 ½ to 2 pounds venison loin, trimmed of all fat
Salt and fresh-ground black pepper to taste
2 tablespoons cognac
2 tablespoons butter, cut into pieces

Preheat the oven to 450°. In a large saucepan, heat 1 tablespoon of the peanut oil and sauté the shallots, mushrooms, peppercorns, bay leaf, and thyme until the mushrooms are browned. Add 1 cup of the Cabernet and reduce to 1 tablespoon over high heat. Add 1 cup of the stock and reduce to a glaze. Add the remaining stock and wine in 3 stages, reducing down until the sauce coats a spoon lightly. Strain through a fine sieve and keep warm.

While the sauce is reducing, prepare the chestnuts. Score the flat side of each chestnut through the shell with a knife. Roast in the preheated oven for 5 minutes, or until the shells are brittle. Remove and peel with a sharp knife while still warm.

Wash and stem the gooseberries and set aside, if using fresh. If using gooseberries in syrup, drain. Frozen gooseberries may be used but should be allowed to thaw at room temperature for 30 minutes before being added to the sauce.

Heat a heavy skillet over high heat and add the remaining 1 tablespoon peanut oil. Season the venison well with salt and pepper. Sauté until well browned on each side and roast in the oven for approximately 8 to 10 minutes, depending on the thickness of the loin. Remove from the oven to a heatproof platter. Reduce the oven temperature to 200°, set the door ajar, and set the platter of venison in the oven to finish cooking, about 10 minutes.

Remove any grease from the skillet and add the cognac. Light it with a match, let it flame, and boil to reduce to a glaze. Add 1 cup of the warm sauce and the chestnuts and bring to a simmer. Remove from the heat, add the gooseberries and the butter, and swirl the pan lightly; adjust the seasoning and keep warm.

Slice the venison with a sharp knife and divide it among 4 heated plates. Spoon the gooseberries and chestnuts equally among the plates along with a small amount of the remaining sauce. Serve immediately.

Baked Apples with Fireweed Honey and Cranberries

Serves 4

With autumn comes a seemingly endless array of varieties of apple from Washington and Oregon. Rome, McIntosh, Northern Spy, Jonathan, Winesap, and Criterion are all outstanding cooking apples, and this dish showcases their beautiful texture and aroma. Fireweed honey is gathered from mountainous areas where the fireweed plant abounds. Its taste is unique: rich, tawny, and spicy. If you can't find it, a wide range of wildflower honeys offers delicious alternatives.

5 large apples
Juice of ½ lemon
¾ to 1 cup cranberries
3 tablespoons sugar
*2 tablespoons raisins, plumped in 3 tablespoons Calvados or
    brandy*
*½ cup raw fireweed honey or any good-quality wildflower
    honey*
1 tablespoon butter
2 pinches ground nutmeg
¼ teaspoon ground cinnamon
2 pinches allspice
Ice cream, whipped cream, or crème fraîche

Preheat the oven to 400°. Preheat the broiler. Peel the apples and leave them whole. Brush with lemon juice and set aside. Place the cranberries on a baking sheet, sprinkle with the sugar, and place in the preheated oven. Bake for 5 to 8 minutes, or until the sugar melts but the cranberries still retain their shape; set aside.

Cut 4 of the apples in half crosswise and hollow out the centers about ½ inch deep, removing the cores and seeds. Reserve any apple pulp. Brush the apples with the lemon juice and set aside. Core the remaining apple and cut into medium dice. Place in a medium saucepan with the reserved pulp, the raisins and Calvados, 2 tablespoons of the honey, the butter, and spices. Cook over low heat for 5 minutes, or until the apples are heated through. Meanwhile, heat the remaining honey in a small saucepan.

Spoon the cooked apples into the apple halves and smooth the surface. Brush each with honey. Arrange the cranberries on top of the apples, brush well with honey, and brush the apples well again.

Bake the apples in the preheated oven for 5 minutes. Baste with the pan juices and more honey. Bake for 5 more minutes, or until the apples are hot. Remove the apples from the oven and brush the cranberries with honey again. Place the apples under the broiler and, watching closely, broil until the cranberries bubble and begin to brown. Remove the apples from the oven, and quickly place each on one of 4 plates, topping each with one fourth of the pan juices. Serve immediately with ice cream, whipped cream, or crème fraîche.

Apple Dumplings

Serves 4

A wonderful autumn treat, especially with homemade ice cream. The attention they require will seem minimal when your fork opens these fragrant, flaky dumplings.

Dough for Pie Crust, page 174
4 Jonathan, Rome, Winesap, or other good-quality, firm
*   cooking apples*
Juice of 2 lemons
¹/₂ cup dry white wine
¹/₃ cup raisins
¹/₄ cup walnuts, chopped coarsely
1¹/₄ teaspoons ground cinnamon
Pinch ground nutmeg
1¹/₂ cups sugar
¹/₄ cup water
¹/₄ cup heavy cream
1 egg
Ice cream, or ¹/₂ cup heavy cream, whipped

Prepare the pie dough and chill well. Peel and core the apples and brush with the lemon juice. In a saucepan, bring the wine to a boil and add the raisins. Remove from the heat and allow the raisins to steep for 20 minutes. Drain the raisins, reserving the wine. Combine the walnuts, raisins, cinnamon, and nutmeg, and moisten with 2 tablespoons of the reserved wine. Fill the apples with this mixture. Combine the remaining wine, the sugar, and water in a medium saucepan and simmer for 5 minutes; keep warm.

Preheat the oven to 400°. Whisk the cream and egg together in a small bowl. Roll the pastry ¹/₈ inch thick between layers of waxed paper into 2 equal-sized squares. Cut each into two 6- or 8-inch squares. Place 1 filled apple in the center of each square. Brush the dough with the egg mixture and bring the corners of the dough up to enclose the apple completely, carefully joining the dough together.

When the apples are all wrapped in dough, roll out the remaining dough and trimmings and cut decorative leaf shapes to place on top of each apple. Brush each apple lightly with the remaining egg wash. Place the apples in a baking dish, allowing plenty of room around each apple.

Bake in the preheated oven for 10 minutes, or until the pastry begins to brown. Turn down the heat to 350° and baste each ap-

ple with 3 tablespoons of the reserved sugar syrup. Bake for 10 minutes and repeat the process. Baste again in 10 minutes with the syrup in the pan. Baste repeatedly until the pastry is browned and crisp and has a shiny glaze, about 10 more minutes.

Carefully remove the apples from the oven and serve immediately with ice cream or whipped cream.

Spiced Figs in Port
with Anjou Pear Ice Cream

Serves 4

The last ripe figs of the season are delicious preserved in port. They will keep for months if refrigerated and are a special treat during the Christmas season. The luscious ice cream is the essence of juicy, fragrant pears, and those of Oregon's Hood River Valley are among the world's finest.

SPICED FIGS IN PORT
12 to 16 Black Mission, Calmyrna, Adriatic, or Kadota figs
1 bottle good-quality port, not too sweet
¹/₂ cup honey
2 bay leaves
1 cinnamon stick
1 teaspoon whole cloves
1 teaspoon minced fresh ginger
12 black peppercorns, crushed, tied in cheesecloth
Zest of ¹/₂ lemon, cut into julienne
Zest of ¹/₂ orange, cut into julienne
2 tablespoons red wine vinegar

ANJOU PEAR ICE CREAM
Custard for Basic Custard Ice Cream, page 179
4 very ripe Anjou, Comice, or Bartlett pears

Sugar Lattice, following
4 mint sprigs
Slices of peeled, cored pear, brushed with lemon
Shortbread Cookies, following (optional)

To make the figs, choose ripe figs that are not bruised or too soft and place them in a glass or ceramic bowl. Combine the port with the honey, herbs, spices, zests and vinegar in a medium-sized non-aluminum saucepan and bring to a boil. Reduce the heat and simmer the liquid for 15 minutes. Remove from the heat and cool to lukewarm. When cooled, pour over the figs. Pierce the figs several times with a fork or paring knife and allow them to macerate for 1 hour.

Strain the port mixture from the figs back into the saucepan and bring to a boil over high heat. Reduce the heat and simmer for about 10 minutes, or until the syrup is shiny and begins to thicken (it should coat the back of the spoon). Remove the syrup from the heat, cool, and pour over the figs. Refrigerate for 2 to 4 hours or, preferably, overnight.

Prepare the custard for the ice cream and let cool. Peel and core the pears while the custard is cooling. Process in a blender or food processor until very smooth. If the pears are not very ripe the puree will appear grainy. Puree again in a blender in small batches if necessary until very smooth.

Combine the cooled custard and the pear puree and freeze according to the manufacturer's instructions for your ice cream machine. Prepare the sugar lattice.

To serve, chill 4 ice cream dishes or dessert plates. Scoop the ice cream onto each dish. Spoon the figs around the ice cream, and garnish with the mint, sugar lattice, and slices of fresh pears.

SUGAR LATTICE
1/2 cup sugar
2 teaspoons water

Cover a baking sheet with waxed paper. Stir the sugar and water in a heavy saucepan over low heat until the sugar is dissolved. Raise the heat to high and cook the sugar, washing down any crystals that form on the sides of the pan with a wet brush, until the syrup reaches 275° on a candy thermometer. Remove the pan from the heat. With a tablespoon, spoon criss-crossing lines of syrup over the waxed paper to form 4 small lattices. Allow to harden for 5 minutes.

Shortbread Nut Cookies

Makes about 4 dozen small cookies

1/2 cup packed brown sugar
1/2 cup (1 stick) butter, softened
2 eggs, beaten
1 teaspoon vanilla or almond extract
2 1/2 cups unbleached all-purpose flour
2 teaspoons baking powder
1/2 teaspoon salt
1 egg
1 tablespoon heavy cream
1 tablespoon sugar
1/3 cup walnuts, almonds, or hazelnuts,* chopped

Preheat the oven to 375°. In a large bowl, cream the brown sugar and butter until light. Add the eggs and the vanilla to the creamed mixture. Sift the flour, baking powder, and salt together and add to the bowl, mixing just until combined.

Chill the dough for 3 to 4 hours. Roll the dough out between sheets of waxed paper and cut it into desired shapes. Beat the egg and cream until combined. Brush the cookie shapes with egg wash and sprinkle with the sugar and chopped nuts. Bake in the preheated oven for 7 to 12 minutes, or until lightly browned, and cool on wire racks.

*If using hazelnuts, toast in a preheated 350° oven for 6 to 8 minutes, then rub off the skins in a kitchen towel or with your palms.

Hazelnut Praline Torte with Espresso Cream

Makes one 10-inch cake, or 12 servings

A fine-textured cake with a creamy, subtly rich buttercream—a coffee lover's dream. Hazelnut trees abound in the Northwest, and this cake is an autumn favorite. It is also wonderful for tea or breakfast, without the buttercream or espresso cream, spread with jam or honey.

1¾ cups hazelnuts

TORTE
1 cup reserved skinned hazelnuts
6 large eggs, at room temperature
¾ cup sugar
1 tablespoon baking powder
1 tablespoon cornstarch
½ cup cake flour
2 tablespoons Frangelico liqueur
½ cup (1 stick) plus 2 tablespoons butter, melted and cooled to lukewarm

BUTTERCREAM
2 cups (4 sticks) unsalted butter, softened
8 egg yolks
¾ cup sugar
2 tablespoons instant espresso powder
½ cup espresso, or 2 tablespoons instant espresso dissolved in ½ cup hot water
3 ounces (3 squares) bittersweet chocolate, melted

ESPRESSO CREAM
¾ cup heavy cream
2 tablespoons sugar
⅓ cup espresso, or 1½ tablespoons instant espresso dissolved in ⅓ cup hot water
2 tablespoons instant espresso powder

1 ounce (1 square) bittersweet chocolate, melted
3 eggs

PRALINE
1 cup sugar
2 tablespoons water
¾ cup reserved skinned hazelnuts

½ cup Frangelico
24 chocolate-covered espresso beans (available in specialty food stores)
Fresh berries for garnish (optional)

Preheat the oven to 350°. Toast the hazelnuts in the preheated oven for 6 to 8 minutes. Remove from the oven, leaving it set at 350°. Rub the skins off the hazelnuts in a kitchen towel or with the palms of your hands. Line the bottom of a 10-inch springform pan with parchment or waxed paper, butter, and dust with flour. Grind the 1 cup peeled hazelnuts in a blender, food processor, or nut grinder until very fine; set aside.

Combine the eggs and sugar in a heatproof bowl and heat over boiling water until the eggs begin to thicken and are warm to the touch. Transfer to a mixing bowl and whip on high speed until the mixture is pale yellow and forms a ribbon when the beater is lifted out of the eggs. Sift the baking powder, cornstarch, and cake flour and fold into the egg mixture, along with the ground hazelnuts, Frangelico, and melted butter.

Pour the batter into the prepared pan and bake in the preheated oven for 35 to 40 minutes, or until a tester inserted in the center comes out clean. Remove from the oven and cool in the pan for 10 minutes before turning out onto a cake rack to cool completely.

To make the buttercream   Whip the butter with a mixer first on low, then on high, until light and creamy. Combine the egg yolks and the sugar in a heatproof bowl. Immerse the bowl in a pan of boiling water and whip constantly until the eggs are very thick and hot, about 5 minutes. Transfer to another bowl set in a bowl of ice and refrigerate until completely cold, about 10 minutes. Set the creamed butter aside at room temperature while the eggs are cooling.

Add the espresso powder to the espresso along with the melted chocolate; stir well and set aside to cool. Slowly whip the chilled egg yolk mixture into the creamed butter. Add the espresso-chocolate liquid and whip on high speed until the mixture is light and creamy; chill.

To make the espresso cream In a small saucepan heat the cream, sugar, espresso, espresso powder, and chocolate until almost boiling. Whisk the eggs in a small bowl until combined, and whisk ½ cup of the hot mixture into the eggs. Whisk the egg mixture into the saucepan and cook over medium heat, whisking constantly until lightly thickened. Pour into a small bowl and chill, whisking occasionally.

To make the praline Place the sugar in a saucepan, stir in the water, and bring to a boil over medium heat. Washing down any crystals that form on the side of the pan with a wet brush, cook the sugar until it caramelizes to a medium amber color. Add all the nuts immediately, stir to combine, and pour the praline onto an oiled baking sheet or marble slab.

Before the praline is thoroughly hardened, separate 12 of the nicest hazelnuts to one side. In about 15 minutes, or when the praline is hardened, break it into pieces and place in a food processor fitted with a metal blade or on a cutting board. Pulse several times and process until the praline is coarsely chopped, or coarsely chop the praline with a sharp knife; set aside.

To assemble the cake Place it on a serving dish and slice it crosswise into 3 even layers with a sharp knife. Brush the bottom layer with Frangelico, spread with buttercream, and sprinkle with praline. Top with another layer and brush with Frangelico. Spread the layer with buttercream and sprinkle with praline. Top with the remaining layer and brush with Frangelico. Spread the buttercream around the top and sides of the cake, reserving about ¼ cup for rosettes. Cover the sides (and the top if you wish) with the ground praline, and pipe 12 rosettes of buttercream around the top with a pastry bag. Garnish each rosette with a chocolate espresso bean and a candied hazelnut.

Spoon the chilled espresso cream onto serving plates and place the sliced cake on top. Garnish the cake with a few fresh berries if desired.

Five-Nut Torte

Serves 12

This dessert requires some advance preparation, but it can be baked 2 days before serving and assembled the day before. The cake is actually better the day after assembly, as the liqueurs, creams, and the nuts all blend and mellow. It's a fine dessert for an elegant dinner or a special occasion.

TORTE
4 ounces (1 cup) hazelnuts
4 ounces (1 cup) pistachios
4 ounces (1 cup) walnuts
4 ounces (¾ cup) blanched slivered almonds
4 ounces (1 cup) pecans
5 tablespoons cornstarch
12 eggs at room temperature
1½ cups sugar
⅓ cup light rum

2 recipes Basic Buttercream, page 177
⅓ cup dark rum, preferably Meyers's
4 ounces (4 squares) bittersweet chocolate, melted
¾ cup Frangelico or Amaretto liqueur
12 each whole hazelnuts, walnut halves, whole pistachios,
   and pecan halves, or 2 tablespoons slivered almonds and
   1 tablespoon powdered sugar

Preheat the oven to 350°. Lightly toast the nuts separately on a baking sheet and cool to room temperature. Rub the skins off the hazelnuts in a kitchen towel or with the palms of your hands. Grind each type of nut separately to a fine powder in a blender, food processor, or nut grinder. Place each type or ground nut in a separate small mixing bowl, adding 1 tablespoon of cornstarch to each bowl. Butter three 10½-by-15½-inch jelly roll pans, line with parchment paper or waxed paper, butter the paper, and coat the pans lightly with flour. Divide one pan in half crosswise with a piece of buttered aluminum foil.

Combine the eggs, sugar, and rum in a large heatproof bowl and whisk immersed in boiling water until heated through. Transfer the warm eggs to the bowl of a mixer and beat at high speed until the mixture is thick and lemon colored and falls in a ribbon when the whip is lifted. Divide the egg mixture evenly among the 5 bowls of nuts. Working quickly and carefully, fold the batter into the nuts; do not overmix.

With a plastic scraper, pour the batters into the baking pans, allowing half of each pan for each nut torte and bringing the batters together in the center. Pour the fifth batter into the buttered half of the divided pan. You will now have 5 separate torte layers. Smooth out the tops, tap gently on the work surface to settle the batter, and bake in the preheated oven for approximately 5 minutes, or until lightly browned and a cake tester inserted in the center comes out clean. Remove the pans to a wire rack and allow the cake to cool in the pans.

The cake can be prepared 2 days ahead up to this point. Wrap each pan well in plastic wrap and leave at room temperature, or freeze if desired.

Prepare the buttercream and divide it equally between 2 bowls, adding the dark rum to one and the melted chocolate to the other. Mix well.

Unmold the torte layers and cut the full layers in half; trim the 5 layers to make 5 even rectangles. Place 1 layer on a serving dish. Brush with the liqueur. Spread a layer of the rum buttercream over the top. Smooth the cream and cover with another torte layer, pressing gently to spread the cream evenly to the edges. Brush the layer with liqueur and spread with a thin layer of chocolate buttercream. Repeat the process, using all 5 torte layers, and ending with chocolate buttercream on top. Do not cover the sides with the buttercream. Chill the cake until very firm, about 1 hour.

The cake can be prepared a day ahead up to this point. Cover it well with plastic wrap, refrigerate overnight, and complete just before serving.

To serve, toast the whole nuts or slivered almonds for garnish in a small skillet in a 350° oven for 5 to 10 minutes, or until lightly browned. Rub the skins off the hazelnuts in a kitchen towel or with the palms of your hands. With a sharp knife, trim each side of the cake neatly to expose the layers. Garnish the cake with rosettes of rum buttercream piped through a pastry bag filled with a star tube. Garnish the rosettes with 1 each of the 5 nuts, or sprinkle the slivered almonds in the center of the cake, and dust lightly with the powdered sugar pushed through a fine sieve. Allow the cake to sit at room temperature for about 15 minutes before serving.

WINTER

WINTER

As autumn's days dwindle, sparked by the bite of frost and coastal winds, winter's light transforms the Northwest. Explosive black clouds swirl over jagged shorelines, pierced by white bolts of sea spray. Forests wrapped in fog glow with winter's bounty: lichen, moss, mountain ash, holly berries, ice-sparkled river rocks. Evergreen boughs dripping in misty rain fill the air with their resiny, comforting scent. Mountain peaks and glaciers crowned with the winter fire of sunset burn with an indigo and orange glow, shooting streamers of color across steel blue clouds.

Although the coastal and mountain storms bring icy winds and snow, the gardens are still alive with cabbages, broccoli, pumpkins, and squashes. And under layers of matted leaves, the earth offers sweet carrots, parsnips, beets, tangy horseradish—simple pleasures, perfect for a winter vegetable soup. Winter greens raised under cover—arugula, mustard, lettuces, mâche—offer salads through the coldest months. What a treat it is to return from the garden with fresh lettuces to enliven a winter meal!

Summer's labors reward us with golden jars of fruits, jams, and preserves, and sweet treasures like raspberries in brandy wait to grace a holiday dessert. While a stern chill grips the days and long nights, the kitchen becomes a source of hearty soups, stews, and chowders. The richness, variety, and flavor of winter's gifts are unique and exciting: festive cakes and cookies; aromatic roasts; oysters, crab, prawns, and salmon, now at their flavors' zenith; the smoky aroma of sausages and fish. We sense the newness of the coming year even as the world is wrapped in darkness—and the kitchen is aglow with family and friends and robust, flavorful foods. Our satisfaction in cooking is fulfilled by simple pleasures, a slower pace, peaceful solitude.

We will be turning the ground soon. Yet, wrapped in winter's magic, we almost want to be held longer in this spell of ice, rain, and heartwarming food.

Now we more deeply understand both our smallness of form and our loftiness of spirit. In the fiercest storm lies a gentle spirit, and the foods of winter are our blessing, these days the embryo of the seasons.

Winter Recipes

Dungeness Crab with Baked Onions and Sea Urchin Butter

Pan-fried Oysters with Herb Fritters and Beet Vinaigrette

Venison Sausage with Sweet Potatoes, Wild Mushrooms, and Quince

Northwest Clam Chowder

Oyster Stew

Roast Onion and Leek Soup with Smoked Salmon Sausage

Gratin of Acorn Squash, Pumpkin, and Bartlett Pears

Sautéed Alaskan Spot Prawns with Roe Butter

Alaskan Scallops with Winter Melon and Black Beans

Sablefish Baked in Parchment with Shiitakes and Marjoram

Halibut Cheeks with Mussels, Cabbage, and Cream of Garlic

Ling Cod with Dungeness Crab, Leeks, and Horseradish

Beef Stew with Dark Beer and Sourdough Dumplings

Roast Lamb with Parsnips, Jerusalem Artichokes, and Dried Apricots

Venison Tenderloin with Satsumas and Ginger

Hot Spiced Red Bartlett Pears with Chocolate Mascarpone and Biscotti

Chestnut-Saffron Marjolaine with Cranberry Mousse and White Chocolate

Christmas Cookies

Alaskan Scallops with Winter Melon and Black Beans

Dungeness Crab with Baked Onions and Sea Urchin Butter

Serves 4

A perfect savory appetizer, light entree, or lunch dish. The onions can be filled with a variety of seafood, and are delicious served chilled with herbed mayonnaise, or mayonnaise with some of the sea urchin roe whipped in. You can also omit the sea urchin butter and serve the onions simply with the butter sauce, or with whole-grain mustard or minced fresh herbs added to the sauce.

8 to 12 boiling onions
8 ounces fresh cooked Dungeness crabmeat
1 shallot, minced
1 tablespoon minced fresh chives
1 teaspoon minced fresh tarragon
Salt, fresh-ground white pepper, and lemon juice to taste
3 tablespoons fresh bread crumbs
½ cup butter (1 stick), melted
White Butter Sauce, page 161
2 to 3 fresh or frozen sea urchin roe, or 1 to 2 anchovy fillets
Minced fresh chives and sea urchin roe for garnish (optional)

Preheat the oven to 400°. Peel the onions and, if large, cut in half. Cut the bottoms flat with a knife and cut a cavity in the center of each onion about ½ to ¾ inch deep. Blanch the onions carefully in simmering salted water for 2 to 3 minutes, or just until tender when pierced with a fork; immerse in ice water, drain, and set aside.

Combine the crabmeat, shallot, and herbs in a small bowl. Season with salt, pepper, and lemon juice. Fill the cavities of the onions equally with the crab mixture. Sprinkle the bread crumbs equally over the crab and brush with the melted butter.

Prepare the White Butter Sauce. Puree the urchin roe or mash well with a fork and whisk into the butter sauce; keep warm. Season the sauce lightly with white pepper; it will need no salt due to the saltiness of the roe.

Place the onions in a baking dish, brush them with the remaining melted butter, and bake in the preheated oven for 5 to 8 minutes, or until the onions are lightly browned and the crab is heated through. Place under the broiler and brown the tops evenly.

Divide the onions equally among 4 preheated plates and spoon a small amount of White Butter Sauce around. Garnish with chives and sea urchin roe if desired, and serve immediately.

Pan-fried Oysters with Herb Fritters and Beet Vinaigrette

Makes 4 appetizer or first-course servings

These crisp, flavorful oysters are equally good as an appetizer or an entree. They are cooked in a matter of seconds and are a delight for oyster lovers. They may even make a few converts.

1 small beet
Basic Vinaigrette, page 165
Salt, pepper, and fresh lemon juice to taste
24 to 32 extra-small Hamma-Hamma, Quilcene, or the best
    local oysters in the shell, or 1 quart shucked oysters
1 cup unbleached all-purpose flour
6 eggs, beaten
2 cups fine dry bread crumbs

HERB FRITTERS
1 tablespoon butter
1 tablespoon minced onion
1 ½ cups unbleached all-purpose flour
1 teaspoon baking powder
½ teaspoon salt
2 large eggs, beaten
1 ½ tablespoons peanut oil
¾ cup milk
1 teaspoon minced fresh parsley
1 teaspoon minced fresh tarragon
2 teaspoons minced fresh chives
Pinch fresh thyme leaves

1 ½ cups peanut oil

Preheat the oven to 350°. Wash the beet well and roast it in the preheated oven until very tender, about 20 to 30 minutes. Cool, peel, and chop the beet coarsely. Prepare the vinaigrette, leaving it in the blender. Add the chopped beet and puree until very smooth. Strain through a fine sieve, adjust the seasoning, and add a light squeeze of lemon juice if necessary; set aside.

Shuck the oysters into a strainer placed over a bowl, reserving all the liquor for other uses in soups, sauces, etc. Dredge the oysters lightly in the flour. Shake off the excess and, one at a time, dip the oysters in the eggs, then the bread crumbs, being careful that the breading adheres evenly to the entire oyster. Place on a platter or baking sheet and, when all oysters are breaded, allow to sit at room temperature for 10 minutes to dry the breading.

Meanwhile, make the herb fritters. Melt the butter in a heavy skillet and sauté the onion until it is translucent. Place the flour, baking powder, and salt in a large bowl. Make a well in the center and add the beaten eggs, the 1 ½ tablespoons peanut oil, and the milk. Stir just to combine. Stir in the onion and herbs. Heat 1 cup of the peanut oil in a heavy skillet until almost smoking and drop the batter by spoonfuls into the oil. Turn and fry on each side and, when golden brown, drain on paper towels and keep warm in the oven.

Pour the remaining ½ cup oil into a skillet large enough to hold half the oysters. Just before the oil begins to smoke, add the oysters. Pan-fry for a few seconds on one side, or just until the breading is golden brown, then turn and fry for another few seconds. Remove with a slotted spoon to a heated platter lined with paper towels; keep warm. Reheat the skillet, adding more oil if necessary, and add the remaining oysters. Pan-fry as for the first panful and, when done, drain on paper towels.

When all the oysters are fried, divide the fritters equally in the center of each of 4 preheated plates. Place the oysters around the fritters and spoon a small amount of the vinaigrette around the oysters. Serve immediately, with extra vinaigrette passed separately.

Venison Sausage with Sweet Potatoes, Wild Mushrooms, and Quince

Serves 4

Game is more readily available in our markets today, and more people are cooking with it. It is very versatile and, if prepared correctly, is an extra-special treat. This sausage is a wonderful appetizer and a perfect way to use venison trim. The recipe will yield more sausage than needed for this dish, but the sausage keeps beautifully and is delicious on its own with crusty bread. If you like, double the recipe and smoke the extra sausages. The sausages will keep for 2 to 3 days in the refrigerator smoked or unsmoked, and they also freeze well.

VENISON SAUSAGE

Makes 4 medium-sized sausages

1½ pounds venison trim from shoulder, leg, etc.
8 ounces pork shoulder
3 ounces pork fat or bacon
2 ounces venison or beef liver
1 cup red wine
¼ cup cognac
1 tablespoon red wine vinegar
2 garlic cloves
2 bay leaves
½ teaspoon ground white pepper, ⅛ teaspoon ground ginger, ⅛ teaspoon ground nutmeg, and ⅛ teaspoon crumbled dried thyme mixed well
⅓ cup shelled pistachios or hazelnuts
2 eggs, beaten

1 medium sweet potato, peeled
3 tablespoons butter
1½ cups wild mushrooms such as chanterelles, cèpes, morels, or shiitakes
½ cup Cabernet Sauvignon wine, or any good-quality dry red wine
1 cup Brown Veal Stock, page 157, or Venison Stock, page 159, or canned low-salt beef broth
1 tablespoon quince jam (available in specialty food stores)
Oil for brushing

Cut the venison, pork shoulder, pork fat, and liver into equal-sized cubes. Place ¾ cup of the red wine, the cognac, vinegar, garlic, and bay leaves in a non-aluminum baking dish. Add the cubed meats, cover, and marinate overnight in the refrigerator.

The next day, drain the meats well, and grind twice through the coarse plate of a food grinder and once through the fine plate. With an electric mixer, or by hand, mix in the remaining ¼ cup red wine, the sausage spices, pistachios, and beaten eggs.

Butter an 18-by-18-inch piece of aluminum foil. Form one quarter of the sausage mixture into a sausage-shaped roll and place in the center of the aluminum foil. Roll the sausage up tightly in the foil, twisting and sealing the ends well. Repeat with each remaining quarter of sausage mixture.

In a saucepan large enough to hold the wrapped sausages, poach them in simmering water to cover for 20 to 25 minutes. (The sausages may also be baked in a preheated 300° oven for 30 to 40 minutes.) Remove and let cool to room temperature. Reserve 3 of the sausages in the refrigerator or the freezer for another use. Refrigerate 1 wrapped sausage for this recipe overnight.

Light a wood or charcoal fire in an open grill, or preheat the broiler. Cut the sweet potato into 1½-inch julienne. Plunge into a saucepan of boiling salted water for 10 seconds, or until three-fourths done. Drain, immerse in ice water, drain again, and set aside.

In a medium skillet over high heat, melt 1 tablespoon of the butter and sauté the wild mushrooms for 1 minute. Add the red wine and boil to reduce to a glaze. Add the stock and reduce until slightly thickened. Whip in the quince jam and 1 tablespoon of the butter. Adjust the seasoning. Slice the sausage into 8 even slices, brush with oil, and grill over high heat for 1 minute. Sauté the sweet potato strips in the remaining 1 tablespoon of butter until lightly browned. Divide the sausage equally among 4 preheated plates, along with the sweet potatoes. Spoon the sauce around and serve immediately.

Northwest Clam Chowder

Serves 4

Summer or winter, clam chowder can always be counted on for sustenance and simple goodness in the Northwest. Its preparation is deceivingly simple. Be careful not to overcook; the chowder should be creamy, light, and have the unmistakable aroma of the sea. Sourdough bread and a light salad make this a perfect winter meal.

3 to 4 pounds Manila, littleneck, or quahog clams, in the
*   shell*
1 cup dry white wine
1 medium potato
½ cup medium-diced yellow onion
½ cup medium-diced celery
2 ounces (1 to 2 slices) bacon, cut into medium dice
2 cups Fish Stock, page 157, or bottled clam juice
1 tablespoon Beurre Manie, page 165
1½ to 2 cups heavy cream
3 tablespoons butter
Salt, pepper, and lemon juice to taste

Wash the clams well, scrubbing with a brush to remove any sand. Place the clams in a large saucepan with a tight-fitting lid, add the white wine, and steam over high heat, shaking the pan occasionally, until the clams open. Strain the clam liquor through cheesecloth; then reduce over high heat to half volume and set aside. Shell the clams and set aside.

Peel the potato, cut it into medium dice, and simmer in salted water to cover until tender but firm, about 3 minutes. Drain and rinse in cold water; set aside.

In a large saucepan, sauté the onion, celery, and bacon until soft; do not allow to brown. Add the clam liquor and fish stock or clam juice and bring to a boil over high heat. Whisk in the *beurre manie* in small amounts, simmer for 5 to 8 minutes, and add the cream and the potato. Return to a boil and simmer for 5 minutes. Add the clams and potato to the chowder. Stir in the butter, salt, pepper, and lemon juice. Serve very hot.

Oyster Stew

Serves 4

There are more recipes for oyster stew than there are cooks. This is one of the best—pure satisfaction. Serve with hot bread or biscuits.

2 tablespoons butter, softened
1½ teaspoons fresh lemon juice
1 teaspoon minced fresh parsley
2¾ to 3 cups heavy cream or milk
24 to 32 very fresh oysters in the shell, preferably Hamma-
*   Hamma, Shoalwaters, Willapa Bays, or Quilcene*
1 shallot, minced
Salt and pepper to taste

Preheat 4 wide-rim soup bowls or crocks. In a medium bowl, beat the butter for 1 minute with a large kitchen spoon. Add the

lemon juice and parsley and beat until the juice is incorporated; set aside. In a large saucepan, bring the cream barely to the simmer; lower the heat. Shuck the oysters into a sieve lined with cheesecloth set over a bowl, reserving all the liquor.

Melt 1 tablespoon of the herb butter in a medium saucepan. When the butter is barely melted, add the shallot and sauté for 10 seconds. Add the oysters all at once, then quickly add the scalded cream mixture and oyster liquor. Adjust the seasoning and immediately divide the stew among the preheated bowls. Serve the remaining herb butter on the side, along with hot bread or biscuits.

Roast Onion and Leek Soup
with Smoked Salmon Sausage

Serves 4

This hearty but light soup is perfect for a gathering of friends on a winter's night and is festive enough for a holiday meal. Both the soup and sausage may be prepared well in advance and finished just before serving.

SAUSAGE
4 ounces boneless salmon
3 egg whites
½ cup heavy cream, chilled
2 ounces Nova or mild-cured smoked salmon
Salt, white pepper, and lemon juice to taste
1 tablespoon minced fresh chives

SOUP
3 to 5 medium yellow onions
1 medium leek, well washed

Olive oil for brushing
2 garlic cloves
6 shallots
3 tablespoons butter
1 tarragon sprig
1 thyme sprig
1 parsley sprig
2 bay leaves
½ teaspoon peppercorns, crushed
2 garlic cloves
*3 or 4 cups Chicken Stock, page 158, or canned chicken
     broth*
¼ cup heavy cream
Pinch each ground nutmeg and cardamom

Olive oil for brushing
Chive, dill, or fennel sprigs for garnish

To make the sausage   Chop the salmon coarsely and puree in a blender or food processor until smooth; add the egg whites and blend until combined. Add the cream all at once and stop as soon as the cream is incorporated. Chop the smoked salmon coarsely and add. Pulse just until the smoked salmon is blended in. Season with salt, pepper, and lemon juice and add the chives.

Lay a 9½-by-11-inch piece of plastic wrap on a work surface and spoon the salmon mixture in the center. Roll the plastic around the salmon to form a sausage and tighten at each end. Roll the sausage in an equal-sized piece of aluminum foil and seal the ends tightly. Place the sausage in a saucepan of near-simmering water and poach for approximately 10 minutes while you prepare the soup.

Preheat the oven to 350°. Rub the onions and leek with olive oil. Place in a baking pan in the preheated oven and roast, turning occasionally, for 30 to 40 minutes, or until the onions are very soft. Add the garlic cloves and 4 of the shallots and continue roasting until the garlic is lightly browned. Remove from the oven and allow to cool.

While the onions are roasting, remove the sausage from the water and cool for 10 minutes. Remove the foil and the plastic wrap, being careful of the hot liquid inside. Remove the sausage carefully to an inverted plate or wire cooling racks, cool, and refrigerate.

Chop the onions when cool enough to handle. In a skillet, heat 1 tablespoon of the butter and sauté the remaining 2 shallots over low heat until lightly browned. Add the roasted onions and the remaining 2 tablespoons of butter. Raise the heat to medium and sauté the onions until they begin to exude their liquid and brown lightly, about 30 minutes. Place the tarragon, thyme, parsley, bay leaves, peppercorns, and 2 garlic cloves on a square of cheesecloth and tie closed with cotton string. Add the chicken stock, the bag of herbs, and the roasted leek, garlic, and shallots.

Simmer the soup for 30 minutes, adding more chicken stock if necessary. Remove the bag of herbs, pressing out all the liquid, and puree the soup in batches in the blender until very smooth. Return to the pot and add the cream, nutmeg, and cardamom.

Meanwhile, preheat the broiler. Slice the sausage into eight ¼-inch slices. Brush with oil and broil until heated through and browned on both sides. Return the soup to a boil and ladle into 4 wide-rim soup bowls. Place 2 sausage slices in each bowl and garnish with chive, dill, or fennel sprigs. Serve immediately.

Note Fennel bulbs are delicious prepared by this method, as are many winter vegetables such as turnips, rutabagas, carrots, and squashes. Adjust the roasting time according to the texture of the vegetable, and be careful not to scorch in the initial roasting period.

Gratin of Acorn Squash, Pumpkin, and Bartlett Pears

Serves 4

All the rich tastes of winter in one dish. This wonderfully aromatic combination is excellent with game and is also an interesting accompaniment to holiday meats.

2 Bartlett pears
1 lemon, halved
3 tablespoons butter
1 tablespoon brown sugar
½ cup honey
2 teaspoons grated fresh ginger
½ teaspoon ground cinnamon
Pinch nutmeg
1 pound fresh pumpkin, peeled, seeded, and diced (about 2 cups)
1 medium acorn squash, peeled, seeded, and diced (about 2 cups)
Salt and pepper to taste
4 eggs
1 cup heavy cream

Preheat the oven to 325°. Peel and core 1 of the pears. Rub it with the cut end of the lemon. Cut the pear into medium dice. Butter a 6-cup gratin dish or casserole with 1 tablespoon of the butter.

In a small skillet, melt the brown sugar and the remaining 2 tablespoons of the butter over medium heat and, when it begins to brown, add the honey. Stirring well, add the ginger, cinnamon, and nutmeg. Remove from the heat. Place 1 layer of mixed pumpkin, squash, and pear in the bottom of the dish and press it down compactly. Brush with the hot honey mixture and sprinkle lightly with salt and pepper; repeat. Or make alternate layers of squash, pumpkin, and pear, brushing with the honey mixture and seasoning with salt and pepper between each layer. Continue until the dish is three-fourths filled, being sure to press the layers down compactly each time.

In a medium bowl, lightly beat the eggs and add the cream, whipping until well blended. Season with salt and pepper and add any remaining honey mixture. Pour the custard over the gratin, shifting the layers carefully with a fork to allow the custard to seep in between. Place the gratin inside a larger pan, add water to halfway up the side of the gratin, and bake in the preheated oven for 15 to 20 minutes, or until a tester inserted in the center comes out clean and the custard is set. Raise the heat to 425° and bake 10 minutes longer to lightly brown the top.

Remove the gratin from the oven and let sit in a warm place for 5 minutes before cutting into serving pieces. Or allow it to completely cool, refrigerate, and then cut into individual portions. Reheat, covered, before serving. Cut the remaining pear into thin slices and divide them among the servings as a garnish.

Roast Onion and Leek Soup with Smoked Salmon Sausage

Sautéed Alaskan Spot Prawns
with Roe Butter

Serves 4

Spot prawns from Alaska (and inland Washington in the Hood Canal) have a taste unmatched by any others: lightly sweet and delicate, yet robust. They should be cooked in the shell, then peeled, for their fullest flavor.

> *24 to 28 spot prawns with roe or large shrimp, in the shell*
> *(about 15 per pound)*
> *White Butter Sauce, page 161*
> *1 teaspoon peanut oil*
> *Salt and pepper to taste*
> *2 tablespoons dry white wine*
> *⅓ cup Fish Stock, page 157, or bottled clam juice*

Carefully remove any roe from the underside of each prawn. Place the roe on a baking sheet. Dry the roe in a preheated 150° oven for 15 to 30 minutes, or until lightly crisp; set aside. Prepare the butter sauce. Whisk the dried roe into the strained sauce. If properly dried, they will remain a vibrant red and soften in the sauce.

In a heavy skillet, heat the peanut oil and sauté the prawns for 1 minute over very high heat, shaking the pan quickly to cook the prawns on all sides. Season with salt and pepper, add the white wine and fish stock, and cover. Steam for 2 minutes. Remove the lid and toss the prawns for 30 seconds to absorb all the liquid. Divide the roe sauce among 4 heated plates and place the prawns in the shell on top. Serve immediately.

Note   If desired, the prawns may be opened with a sharp knife through the undershell just before serving. This will make it easier to remove the shells from the prawns at the table.

Alaskan Scallops
with Winter Melon and Black Beans

Serves 4

Scallops from the Arctic waters of Alaska are at their best in winter, tasting of the sweet essence of the sea. Winter melon is a pearly white, delicate member of the squash family used in Asian soups. Black beans give this preparation a unique rich flavor.

> *⅔ to ¾ cup dried black beans*
> *1½ pounds Alaskan, Pacific, or eastern sea scallops (about 12*
> *to a pound)*
> *8 ounces winter melon (available in Asian markets)*
> *Salt and pepper to taste*
> *2 garlic cloves, crushed*
> *1 tablespoon peanut oil*
> *¼ cup dry white wine*
> *½ to 1 teaspoon black bean paste (available in Asian*
> *markets)*
> *2 tablespoons butter*
> *Fresh lemon juice to taste*

Sauteed Alaskan Spot Prawns with Roe Butter

Wash the dried black beans and soak them in cold water to cover overnight. Dry the scallops well and slice in half crosswise; set aside. Remove the seeds and peel from the winter melon. Slice the melon into 16 to 20 thin slices, cover, and refrigerate.

Drain the soaked beans. In a small saucepan, cover the black beans with cold water, season with salt and pepper, and add the crushed garlic. Bring to a boil, reduce to a simmer, and cook the beans until tender, about 20 minutes. Discard the garlic cloves; drain the beans and keep warm.

Heat a large skillet over high heat. When it begins to smoke, add 1 teaspoon of the peanut oil and the winter melon slices. Season with salt and pepper and brown well on one side. Re-move to a platter and keep warm. Reheat the pan and, when it begins to smoke, add 1 teaspoon of the peanut oil and half of the scallops. Sear the scallops well on one side until lightly browned, about 15 seconds. Remove to a platter and keep warm. Sear the remaining scallops on one side in the remaining teaspoon of oil; remove and keep warm. Add the wine to the skillet and reduce by half. Whisk in the black bean paste. Remove from the heat and whisk in the butter. Adjust the seasoning with pepper and lemon juice (the sauce will need no salt).

Arrange the winter melon slices in a fan on each of 4 preheated plates. Place the scallops around the slices and garnish with a spoonful of the black beans. Spoon the sauce around the scallops and serve immediately.

Sablefish Baked in Parchment with Shiitakes and Marjoram

Serves 4

Sablefish, or black cod, is a delicious fish, with a rich flesh that is excellent for smoking or roasting. Baked in parchment and paired with aromatic shiitakes and marjoram, smoked sablefish is fine winter fare. Sablefish is also delicious prepared this way unsmoked, as is red rockfish, quillbacked rockfish, Pacific snapper, yellowtail rockfish, black sea bass, or any firm-fleshed fish. You will need 4 sheets of baking parchment, each 12 by 18 inches. Seal the packets well and be sure not to overcook the fish.

8 ounces shiitakes, or 2 ounces dried mushrooms
  reconstituted in ½ cup dry white wine
5 tablespoons butter

2 tablespoons Marsala
8 to 12 new potatoes
Four 6-ounce fillets smoked sablefish or any firm, white-
  fleshed fish
4 marjoram sprigs
4 or 8 garlic cloves
Dry white wine to taste
Balsamic vinegar to taste
Salt and fresh-ground white pepper to taste

Slice the shiitakes ¼ inch thick. In a skillet, melt 1 tablespoon of the butter and sauté the shiitakes over high heat for 30 seconds, then add the Marsala and sauté until absorbed; remove from the heat and set aside. Simmer the new potatoes in lightly salted water to cover for 10 to 12 minutes, or until tender. Rinse in cold water and set aside.

Preheat the oven to 400°. Crease four 12-by-18-inch sheets of parchment in the middle and place a fillet on the bottom half nearest you. Divide the shiitakes equally among the 4 fillets and place a marjoram sprig on top of each, along with 1 or 2 garlic

Sablefish Baked in Parchment with Shiitakes and Marjoram

cloves. Dot each fillet with 1 tablespoon of butter, sprinkle with white wine and balsamic vinegar, and season with salt and white pepper. Place a few new potatoes in each packet and fold the top crease over the fish. Beginning with one corner, fold the edges over tightly all the way around the packets, twisting well and folding the last corner under at the end.

Bake the packets in the preheated oven for about 12 minutes, or 10 minutes per inch of the thickness of the fillets, or until the packets are well inflated. Serve the packets immediately on preheated individual plates, to be opened at the table.

Halibut Cheeks with Mussels, Cabbage, and Cream of Garlic

Serves 4

While salmon is prized worldwide, the flavor of halibut from icy Northwest waters is not to be missed. It is full-bodied yet light, rich but not overpowering. The cheeks—tender, rich sections above the jaw—are moist and flavorful, with a texture similar to shellfish. This dish offers the heartiness and deep-down satisfaction of a seafood stew, yet it is both light and subtle.

4 halibut cheeks, or halibut or any firm white-fleshed fish
fillets (1½ pounds total)
½ head green cabbage
½ head red cabbage
Salt and pepper to taste
Vin Blanc Sauce, page 162
12 to 20 garlic cloves
1 pound mussels, scrubbed and debearded
½ cup dry white wine

2 tablespoons butter
4 thyme sprigs
2 tablespoons dry red wine
Lemon juice to taste

If they are larger than the inside of your palm, slice the halibut cheeks in half on the bias. Select 4 to 6 of the most attractive leaves of the green cabbage, reserving the remaining cabbage for other dishes. Blanch each leaf in rapidly boiling salted water for 5 seconds and immerse immediately in ice water; dry well and set aside. Pull 4 to 6 leaves from the red cabbage and shred them very fine; set aside. Season each of the cheeks with salt and pepper and wrap each one in a blanched green cabbage leaf; set aside.

Prepare the Vin Blanc Sauce and set aside. Cover the garlic cloves with cold water in a small saucepan. Bring to a boil and drain immediately. Repeat the process twice more, then drain the garlic cloves and set aside. Reserve 8 to 12 of the nicest cloves for garnish. Puree the remaining blanched garlic cloves with the Vin Blanc Sauce until smooth; adjust the seasoning and set aside.

Place the halibut cheeks, mussels, and white wine in a skillet with a tight-fitting lid. Dot each cheek with a small piece of butter and add the thyme sprigs and the reserved garlic cream. Cover the pan and steam gently over medium heat for 3 to 4 minutes, or until the mussels open. High heat will toughen the cheeks. Remove the cheeks and mussels to a warm platter and keep warm. Return the liquid in the pan to a boil and reduce until lightly thickened. Return the cheeks and mussels to the pan and keep warm. Steam the reserved red cabbage slices in 2 tablespoons red wine for 1 minute, or until al dente; season with salt, pepper, and lemon juice.

Slice 3 or 4 slices from each cabbage-wrapped cheek. Arrange the remaining piece of each cheek on each of 4 plates with the mussels and arrange the slices around. Spoon some of the sauce onto each plate along with a small amount of red cabbage. Sprinkle with the reserved blanched garlic cloves and serve immediately.

Ling Cod with Dungeness Crab, Leeks, and Horseradish

Serves 4

Ling cod, caught by the long-line method whereby each fish is individually handled as opposed to being damaged in large nets, is one of the finest fish in the Pacific. Firm-fleshed, moist, and full-flavored, it makes a heartwarming dish when combined with succulent Dungeness crab.

1 tablespoon minced fresh chives
4 teaspoons fine dry bread crumbs
1 teaspoon minced garlic
Light squeeze of lemon juice
1 tablespoon minced shallot
4 ounces fresh cooked Dungeness crabmeat, drained
1 egg yolk
Salt and white pepper to taste
1 medium leek, white part only
One 2-inch-long piece fresh horseradish root
Four 6-ounce ling cod fillets, long-line caught preferably, or
  true cod, black cod, eastern cod, or scrod fillets
¼ cup dry white wine
3 tablespoons heavy cream
4 tablespoons butter, cut into pieces
8 to 12 chives for garnish

Preheat the oven to 400°. Combine the chives, bread crumbs, garlic, lemon juice, and shallot in a small mixing bowl. Add the crab meat and the egg yolk. Toss lightly, just until the ingredients are combined. Season and refrigerate.

Wash the leek and cut into julienne; you should have about 1 cup. Cut the horseradish into julienne; you should have ½ cup. Mince enough of the horseradish to make 1 teaspoon and reserve. Cover the remaining horseradish with cold water in a small saucepan, bring to a simmer, and drain. Repeat the process twice more and cool the horseradish in ice water; drain and set aside.

Slice the ling cod into 4 equal-sized serving pieces. Make a 2-inch-long diagonal slice about ½ inch deep in each fillet. Fill each cavity with an equal amount of the crab mixture; season the fillets.

Place the fillets in a skillet just large enough to hold them, and add the white wine, the blanched horseradish, and the leeks. Bring to a simmer on top of the stove, cover, and bake in the preheated oven for approximately 5 minutes. The fish should be slightly underdone, still soft to the touch.

Remove the ling cod from the pan and keep warm. Boil the pan juices over high heat to reduce by half, add the cream, and reduce until thickened. Add the reserved minced horseradish to taste. Horseradish varies greatly in hotness, so be careful, tasting after each addition. Whip in the butter in pieces and adjust the seasoning.

Place the leek and horseradish julienne in the center of 4 preheated plates. Place a fillet on top of each and spoon the horseradish sauce around. Garnish the top of each fillet with chives, and serve immediately.

Beef Stew with Dark Beer and Sourdough Dumplings

Serves 4

Beef stews like this one have simmered over western campfires for more than a century, since the days when white men and women first crossed the mountains. These dumplings, from an old camp cook, will raise the lid right off the kettle.

Beef Stew with Dark Beer and Sourdough Dumplings

2 or 2½ cups unbleached all-purpose flour
½ cup Sourdough Starter, page 170
¼ to ½ cup milk

STEW
2 tablespoons peanut oil
Salt and pepper to taste
1½ to 2½ pounds beef stew meat, preferably chuck
3 to 4 shallots, minced
3 garlic cloves, minced
1 medium onion, minced
2 bottles Guinness stout, or any good-quality dark beer
2 quarts Brown Veal Stock, page 157, or low-salt canned beef broth
1 teaspoon crushed black peppercorns, 3 bay leaves, 4 cloves, 2 parsley sprigs, and 3 thyme sprigs, tied in a cheesecloth bag
2 Idaho russet potatoes, peeled and quartered, or 12 new potatoes
2 medium turnips, quartered
2 medium carrots, peeled and cut into chunks
1½ cups pearl onions, or 4 boiling onions

1 tablespoon baking powder
½ teaspoon salt
3 eggs, beaten
2 tablespoons minced fresh parsley

To make the dumplings, sift 1 cup of the flour into a large mixing bowl. Add the sourdough starter and the milk, and stir to combine. Allow to rest for about 1 hour while you prepare the stew.

Heat the oil in a heavy saucepan, soup pot, or, preferably, a cast-iron kettle. When it begins to smoke, season the meat and sear it over high heat until evenly browned. Remove the meat from the pan and set aside. Lower the heat and sauté the shallots, garlic, and the onion until evenly browned, about 1 minute. Add one bottle of the stout and boil to reduce by half. Add 1 cup of the veal stock and reduce again, this time by two thirds.

Repeat the process twice more, add the remaining stout, skimming off any impurities, and reduce again until very thick. Add the remaining stock and reduce again until the sauce is still slightly thin. Add the seared meat and the bag of herbs, and simmer the stew over low heat for 45 minutes to 1 hour, or until the meat is almost tender.

Add the potatoes and simmer for about 10 more minutes. Add the turnips and the carrots and simmer 5 to 10 minutes. When all the vegetables are three-fourths done, add the pearl onions; keep warm.

To finish the dumplings, sift 1 cup of the flour and the baking powder and salt into the starter and add the eggs and parsley; you should have a thick batter. Do not overmix. Sift an additional ½ cup flour into the dumpling mix if it is too thin.

Spoon the batter over the top of the stew with a tablespoon and cover the pot. Steam the dumplings over low heat for 8 to 10 minutes, or until a tester inserted in the middle of a dumpling comes out clean. Remove from the stew and keep warm.

Return the stew to a simmer and adjust the seasoning. Divide among heated wide-rim soup bowls with the dumplings on top, or serve the stew and dumplings directly from the pot.

Roast Lamb with Parsnips, Jerusalem Artichokes, and Dried Apricots

Serves 4

The caramelized parsnips, Jerusalem artichokes, and dried apricots lend a mellow sweetness to the hardiness of lamb. This dish is also very good prepared with turnips, and with other cuts of meat such as roast leg of lamb, lamb chops, lamb racks, and lamb shoulder.

2 dried apricots
¾ cup dry red wine
1 teaspoon peanut oil
One 1½-pound lamb loin, trimmed of all fat, at room
*   temperature*
3 garlic cloves
2 thyme sprigs
3 tablespoons butter
3 medium parsnips
2 medium Jerusalem artichokes
1 tablespoon sugar
Lamb Natural Juice, page 159
Salt and pepper to taste

Preheat the oven to 450°. Place the apricots in the wine to soak for 15 minutes. Peel the parsnips and cut them into ½-inch-thick rounds; set aside. Remove the apricots from the wine, reserving the wine, and cut the apricots into julienne strips; set aside.

Heat a heavy skillet over high heat, add the peanut oil, and sear the lamb well on all sides. Add the garlic cloves and herb sprigs and roast in the oven, turning often, for 8 to 10 minutes, or until medium rare.

While the lamb is roasting, prepare the vegetables. Heat 1 tablespoon of the butter in a large heavy skillet until foamy. Add the vegetables, raise the heat to high, and brown on both sides, in separate batches if necessary. When the vegetables are well browned, sprinkle lightly with the sugar and turn frequently as the sugar caramelizes. When the vegetables are amber brown, add ¼ cup of the Natural Juice, being careful of splattering, and boil to reduce until the vegetables absorb all the juices. The vegetables should be a rich brown, tender but firm. Remove to a platter and keep warm. Clean the skillet and repeat with remaining vegetables, if necessary using the last tablespoon of butter and the remaining ¼ cup Natural Juice; keep warm.

Remove the lamb from the skillet and keep warm. Add the red wine from the apricots to the lamb roasting pan, scraping any browned bits from the bottom, and boil to reduce to a glaze.

Add all but ¼ cup of the remaining Natural Juice and boil to reduce until the sauce lightly coats a spoon. Strain, whisk in 1 tablespoon of the butter, and adjust the seasoning.

Just before serving, add the julienne strips of apricot to the vegetables, reheat, and adjust the seasoning. Arrange the vegetables and apricot strips on 4 preheated plates. Slice the lamb and divide among the plates on top of the slices. Spoon a small amount of the sauce around and serve immediately.

Venison Tenderloin
with Satsumas and Ginger

Serves 4

This dish combines the richness of Northwest game with the flavors of the Pacific Rim. Satsumas, seedless Asian tangerines, are one of the treats of winter, and their sweetness coupled with the tang of ginger adds a unique taste to venison.

One 1½-pound venison tenderloin, trimmed of all fat
3 satsumas or tangerines
2 shallots, chopped
5 mushrooms, chopped
2 tablespoons peanut oil
2 tablespoons soy sauce or tamari
¼ teaspoon black peppercorns, crushed
1 teaspoon dried orange peel (available in Asian markets), or
*   1 teaspoon grated fresh orange zest*
1 teaspoon dried lily flowers, optional (available in Asian
*   markets)*
1 garlic clove, chopped
3 thyme sprigs

[133]

Venison Tenderloin with Satsumas and Ginger

3 cups Venison Stock, page 159, Brown Veal Stock, page 157,
*   or low-salt canned beef broth*
Candied Ginger, page 178
Salt and pepper to taste

Preheat the oven to 450°.

Allow the venison tenderloin to sit at room temperature for 10 minutes. Cut 1 of the satsumas in half; peel and section the remaining 2.

In a large skillet, sauté the shallots and mushrooms in 1 tablespoon of the peanut oil until browned. Add the juice of the halved satsuma to the pan and boil to reduce by half. Add the soy sauce, peppercorns, dried orange peel, dried lily flowers, garlic, and thyme to the pan and bring to a boil. Add ½ cup of the stock and boil to reduce by half. Add the remaining stock and boil to reduce until the sauce lightly coats a spoon. Add 1 teaspoon of the syrup from the candied ginger and return to a boil. Strain through a fine sieve, pressing out all the liquid, and set the sauce aside.

Season the venison with salt and pepper. In a heavy skillet, heat the remaining tablespoon of peanut oil and sear the venison over high heat until well browned. Roast in the oven for 10 to 12 minutes for medium rare. Remove the roast to a heated platter and keep warm.

Discard any fat from the skillet and add ¼ cup of the sauce. Boil to reduce by half and add the remaining sauce. Keep warm. Toss the satsumas with the candied ginger and divide among 4 heated plates. Slice the venison and divide it among the 4 plates. Spoon a small amount of sauce around. Serve immediately.

Hot Spiced Red Bartlett Pears
with Chocolate Mascarpone and Biscotti

Serves 4

Bartletts are delicious when picked in late autumn and allowed to ripen in a cool, dark place. Red Bartletts are ideal for poaching, as their flesh is firm and flavorful. It's fun to improvise on the poaching liquid with a variety of flavorings: lavender honey, geranium leaves, herbs such as basil and thyme, and the wide range of liqueurs. This dessert is equally delicious served chilled, or baked in individual tarts (bake tart shells, page 175, fill with the mascarpone, and top with the sliced pears). A glass of the dessert wine used in the poaching liquid really tops off this dessert. Be sure to save the poaching liquid; this is a wonderful way to preserve poached pears or other fruits, either by canning them in the liquid or refrigerating them in the liquid in tightly covered jars.

SPICED PEARS
2½ cups Sauternes, late-harvest Riesling, or any good-
*   quality dessert wine*
½ cup sugar
½ vanilla bean, slit open lengthwise
Zest of ½ lemon, cut into strips
Two 2½-inch-long strips orange zest
4 cloves, 2 bay leaves, ½ teaspoon crushed black
*   peppercorns, and 1 thyme sprig tied in a cheesecloth bag*
⅛ teaspoon ground nutmeg
Pinch ground mace
3 pinches ground cardamom

1 cinnamon stick
2 to 3 scented geranium leaves (optional)
4 firm, ripe Red Bartlett, Bartlett, Anjou, or Comice pears
*   with stems*

CHOCOLATE MASCARPONE
4 to 6 ounces fresh mascarpone cheese
3 tablespoons powdered sugar
3 ounces (3 squares) bittersweet chocolate, melted
1 teaspoon dark rum or liqueur of choice

2 tablespoons butter, melted
2 tablespoons walnuts, coarsely chopped
Biscotti, following

Preheat the oven to 450°. To make the spiced pears, combine all of the ingredients except the pears in a large non-aluminum saucepan and bring to a boil. Simmer uncovered for 15 minutes. With a paring knife, cut three ¾-inch-wide bands lengthwise from the skin of each pear to make alternating red and white strips. Add the pears to the liquid, cover, and reduce the heat to very low. Gently cook the pears 2 to 3 minutes, remove from heat, and allow to sit covered for 5 minutes. The cooking time will vary greatly depending on the ripeness of the fruit. It is best to test the pears for doneness with a metal or bamboo skewer. They should be tender but firm. Remove the pears from the syrup and allow them to cool to room temperature on wire racks. Chill the syrup on ice and, when completely cooled, add the pears, cover, and refrigerate for 4 hours or overnight.

To make the chocolate mascarpone, whip the mascarpone with the powdered sugar until smooth. Cool the melted chocolate and add to the cheese along with the rum. Whisk well and refrigerate until firm. Spoon into a pastry bag fitted with a star tube; set aside.

Preheat the oven to 450°. Remove the pears from the syrup and drain. Cut the bottoms flat with a knife, then cut off the stem with approximately 1 inch of the pear attached and set aside. With a teaspoon or melon baller, carefully hollow the pears out, removing the core. Place each pear in an ovenproof skillet large enough to hold all 4 without crowding and brush with the melted butter.

Bake in the preheated oven for 5 minutes or until the pears are barely heated through. Remove the skillet to the top of the stove and, with tongs, carefully turn each pear over in the hot butter to lightly brown. Remove to warm serving plates. Using the pastry bag, fill each whole pear with the mascarpone. Place the tops back on the pears and sprinkle with the chopped nuts. Serve immediately with the biscotti.

BISCOTTI

Makes 18 cookies

1¼ cups unbleached all-purpose flour

1 large egg

1 cup sugar

1½ teaspoons fresh grated orange zest

2 tablespoons anisette or Pernod

3 tablespoons rum or brandy

¾ cup hazelnuts, almonds, or a combination, coarsely chopped

1 teaspoon baking powder

Preheat the oven to 350°. Oil and flour a large baking sheet. In a large bowl, combine the flour, egg, sugar, zest, anisette, and rum. Beat until thoroughly blended. If using hazelnuts, toast them in the oven for 6 to 8 minutes, then rub off the skins in a kitchen towel or with your palms. Beat the nuts and baking powder into the dough.

Shape half of the dough into a sausage shape and place on the baking sheet. Repeat with the remaining dough, allowing room for the dough to spread when baked.

Bake in the preheated oven for 1 hour. Remove from the oven and cool on the pan for 20 minutes, then run a spatula under-neath the pastries to loosen. Let cool to room temperature so they will slice easily.

Cut each pastry into crosswise slices about 1 inch thick. Arrange the slices on baking sheet and return to a preheated 350° oven for about 10 minutes. Cool and store in airtight containers.

Chestnut-Saffron Marjolaine with Cranberry Mousse and White Chocolate

Makes 12 servings

Inspired by the traditional Swedish saffron tea cake, this special-occasion dessert is a show-stopper. Don't be over-whelmed by the number of steps. All the parts can be prepared in advance and the cake assembled a few hours before serving. It keeps remarkably well and is also delicious served unadorned for tea.

CAKE

½ teaspoon saffron

¼ cup milk

38 chestnuts

⅔ cup chestnut flour (available in specialty food stores; see page 181), or increase the following cake flour to ¾ cup

⅔ cup cake flour

2 teaspoons baking powder

¼ teaspoon ground ginger

¼ teaspoon ground nutmeg

Pinch ground mace

Pinch ground cardamom

6 eggs, at room temperature

¾ cup sugar

Chestnut-Saffron Marjolaine with Cranberry Mousse and White Chocolate

¾ cup (1½ sticks) butter, melted
½ teaspoon fresh lemon juice
½ teaspoon vanilla extract
1 tablespoon dark rum

MERINGUE
¼ cup reserved chopped chestnuts
1 teaspoon cornstarch
7 egg whites, at room temperature
Pinch salt
1⅓ cups sugar

WHITE CHOCOLATE GANACHE
8 ounces white chocolate
½ cup heavy cream
1 tablespoon butter

CRANBERRY MOUSSE
1 cup cranberries
½ cup water
¼ cup sugar
2 teaspoons plain gelatin
1 tablespoon cold water
1 cup heavy cream

2 tablespoons dark rum
2 ounces white chocolate for garnish
Powdered sugar for dusting

CANDIED CHESTNUTS
1 cup sugar
2 tablespoons water
8 reserved whole chestnuts

Preheat the oven to 375°. Have all the ingredients at room temperature. Line the bottom of a 12-by-18-inch baking sheet with parchment or waxed paper. Butter and flour the bottom and sides, shaking out the excess flour. Soak the saffron in the milk for 15 minutes.

Cut an X into each chestnut with a sharp knife and roast in the preheated oven until the shells are brittle. Remove from the oven and peel while still warm; do not turn off the oven. Reserve 8 of the nicest chestnuts for garnish. Chop the remaining nuts coarsely; return them to the oven and continue to roast them until they are lightly browned. Remove the nuts from the oven, lowering the oven temperature to 350°. Cool and chop the nuts coarse. Reserve ¼ cup of the chopped chestnuts.

Sift the dry ingredients and spices into a mixing bowl. Beat the eggs and sugar over low heat until warmed and transfer to an electric mixer. Beat on high speed until the mixture is thick and forms a ribbon when the beater is lifted. Fold the dry ingredients into the egg mixture alternately with the melted butter and the saffron milk. Fold in the lemon juice, vanilla, and the rum; mix swiftly and lightly.

Pour the batter into the prepared pan and bake at 350° for 15 to 18 minutes, or until a tester inserted in the center of the cake comes out clean. Cool on a wire rack for 5 minutes, and unmold the cake onto the wire rack to cool. (The cake may be prepared ahead up to this point, then wrapped in plastic wrap and held in a cool, dry place or frozen if desired.)

To make the meringue   Reduce the oven temperature to 225°. Combine the reserved chopped chestnuts and cornstarch. Whip the egg whites and salt to stiff peaks. Slowly beat in the sugar and continue beating until the whites are smooth and stiff. Carefully fold in the chopped chestnuts. Butter a piece of parchment or waxed paper to fit a cookie sheet. Spoon the meringue into a pastry bag with a No. 4 plain tip and pipe lines into a solid 12-by-4-inch rectangle on the sheet. Dry in the 225° oven until crisp, about 1 hour. Cool on a wire rack. (This may be prepared 1 to 2 days ahead, wrapped in plastic wrap, and stored in a cool, dry place.)

To make the ganache   Chop the white chocolate fine. In a medium saucepan, heat the cream until almost boiling and stir in the chocolate. Stir slowly, adding the butter, until smooth and glossy. Refrigerate until set.

To make the cranberry mousse   In a medium saucepan, simmer the cranberries, water, and sugar until tender, about 10 minutes. Puree in a blender or food processor until very smooth and transfer to a bowl. Soften the gelatin in the cold water and mix into the cranberry mixture; refrigerate for 15 minutes. Whip the cream to soft peaks and fold into the puree; refrigerate.

To assemble the cake   Cut the cake into two 4-inch-wide pieces, reserving all trim (see Note, below). Brush the cake with the rum. Place 1 strip on the bottom of a serving dish. Smooth a ¼-inch layer of white chocolate ganache over the cake layer. Place a layer of meringue on top. Spread a layer of cranberry mousse on the meringue. Place another cake layer on top and press firmly. Smooth the sides of the cake with ganache, using a spatula. Lightly press down on the top layer.

Grate the 2 ounces white chocolate coarsely and press it into the sides and top of the cake. Cover the cake with plastic wrap and freeze for 6 hours or overnight. Cut the cake into equal serving pieces and dust each with powdered sugar. Refrigerate for 1 hour.

Meanwhile, prepare the candied chestnuts. Dissolve the sugar and water in a small saucepan. Cook over medium-high heat, washing down any crystals from the side of the pan with a wet brush, until the syrup reaches 275° on a candy thermometer and is amber brown. Place each chestnut on a bamboo skewer and immerse each one in the syrup, covering the chestnut well. Slowly lift the chestnut from the syrup, allowing long threads of caramel to harden. Place the skewers on the edge of a work surface with a weight on top so that the caramel strands hang over the edge. When ready to serve, remove from the skewers and place on the cake.

Note   A delicious trifle can be made with the reserved trim by brushing the cake pieces with liqueur and layering them in a bowl with pear slices, peach slices, or berries, and custard.

Christmas Cookies

These cookies will become your absolute favorites as soon as you prepare them. I know of no one who has enjoyed these treats without smiling.

Chocolate Fudge Fingers

Makes about 7 dozen cookies

3 eggs
¾ cup granulated sugar
⅓ cup brown sugar
1 tablespoon brandy
1 teaspoon vanilla extract
¾ cup (1½ sticks) butter, melted
1¼ cups cocoa
1 cup unbleached all-purpose flour
¼ teaspoon baking powder
¼ teaspoon salt
4 ounces walnuts, pecans, or almonds, minced (about 1 cup)
2 tablespoons powdered sugar
2 tablespoons cocoa

Preheat the oven to 350°. Combine the eggs, granulated sugar, brown sugar, brandy, and vanilla extract in a medium bowl and beat at medium speed until smooth. Add the melted butter slowly and continue mixing at medium speed until incorporated; set aside.

Sift together the cocoa, flour, baking powder, and salt. Combine the sifted dry ingredients with the egg-sugar mixture in the bowl and blend until combined. Add the minced nuts.

Spread the mixture evenly in a greased 9-by-13-inch baking

pan and bake in the preheated oven for 15 to 20 minutes, or until firm. Cool the cookies in the pan on a wire rack until just warm. Cut into fingers ¾ inch wide by 2 inches long. Sift together the powdered sugar and cocoa. Roll the cookies in the sweetened cocoa to coat them evenly. Store in a tightly covered container in a cool, dry place.

Pecan Peppernuts

Makes about 6 dozen cookies

4 eggs
2 cups sugar
4 cups unbleached all-purpose flour
1 teaspoon baking powder
¼ teaspoon salt
2 teaspoons ground cinnamon
½ teaspoon ground black pepper
½ teaspoon ground cloves
Grated zest of 1 lemon
Grated zest of ½ orange
¼ teaspoon anise seeds, crushed
¼ cup golden raisins, minced
½ cup pecans, minced

GLAZE
3 egg whites
1½ tablespoons honey
1½ teaspoons orange liqueur
½ teaspoon anise seeds, crushed
3 cups sifted powdered sugar

About 72 pecan halves for garnish

Preheat the oven to 350°. In a medium bowl, beat the eggs on high speed until light and lemon colored. Beat in the sugar gradually, then beat 10 minutes longer. Meanwhile, sift together the flour, baking powder, salt, cinnamon, black pepper, and cloves. Add to the egg mixture and blend to combine. Add the lemon and orange zests and the anise seeds, raisins, and nuts. Turn the mixture out on a lightly floured work surface and knead lightly for 10 seconds.

Cover and chill the mixture overnight or up to 48 hours to blend the flavors. Allow the dough to rest out of the refrigerator until it reaches room temperature. On a lightly floured surface, roll out ½ inch thick. Cut into 1-inch circles. Place on a lightly greased baking sheet and bake in the preheated oven for 12 to 15 minutes. Cool on a wire rack.

To make the glaze, blend the egg whites, honey, orange liqueur, and anise seeds. Beat in the powdered sugar. Dip the cookies into the glaze and allow to dry on waxed paper. Before the glaze hardens, top each cookie with a pecan half.

Cream Cheese Spritz Leaves

Makes about 5 dozen cookies

1 cup (2 sticks) butter, softened
4 ounces cream cheese, at room temperature
1 cup sugar
1 egg, slightly beaten
1 tablespoon orange liqueur
1 teaspoon finely grated orange zest (optional)
2¼ to 2½ cups unbleached all-purpose flour
1 teaspoon baking powder
6 ounces (6 squares) semisweet chocolate

Preheat the oven to 375°. In a medium bowl, cream the butter, cream cheese, and sugar until smooth. Add the egg, orange liqueur, and zest and blend well. Add the flour and baking powder; blend well. Chill the dough for 30 minutes.

Using a cookie press, press the dough out into leaves or into other desired shapes on ungreased baking sheets. Bake in the preheated oven for 8 minutes, or until just barely beginning to brown; cool on wire racks.

Melt the semisweet chocolate over hot water. Dip the bottoms of the cookies into the chocolate and allow to set on waxed paper.

Nut Shortbread Jam Bars

Makes about 7 dozen cookies

CRUST
¾ pound hazelnuts
3 cups unbleached all-purpose flour
1½ cups sugar
1½ cups (3 sticks) butter, cut in ¼-inch cubes and chilled
2 eggs, beaten
Grated zest of 1 lemon
1½ to 2 cups high-quality jam or preserves (to make your own, see Note, below)

TOPPING
1 cup unbleached all-purpose flour
½ cup sugar
½ cup nuts, chopped
½ cup (1 stick) chilled butter, cut in ¼-inch cubes
Powdered sugar for dusting

Preheat the oven to 350°. Toast the hazelnuts in the oven for 6 to 8 minutes, then rub off the skins in a kitchen towel or with your palms. Grind the hazelnuts fine in a blender, food processor, or nut grinder. Combine the flour and sugar in a medium bowl, and cut the chilled butter cubes into the flour mixture with your fingers, a pastry cutter, or 2 knives, until the dough

resembles coarse oatmeal. Add the hazelnuts; stir to combine. Add the eggs and lemon zest, mixing until the dough forms a loose ball; refrigerate.

Press the chilled dough ¼ inch thick into the bottom and sides of a 10½-by-15½-inch buttered jelly roll pan. Pour the jam over the dough, spreading it evenly.

To make the topping, combine the flour, sugar, and nuts in a medium bowl (if using hazelnuts, skin as in paragraph one). Cut the butter into the flour mixture with your fingers, a pastry cutter, or 2 knives until the mixture resembles coarse meal. Sprinkle this mixture over the jam.

Bake the cookies in the preheated oven for 10 to 12 minutes, or until the topping is evenly browned. Cool the pan on a wire rack and, when cooled, cut into 1-by-2-inch bars. Dust lightly with powdered sugar. Store in a tightly covered container in a cool, dry place.

Note For a simple homemade fruit jam, simmer 2 pounds fresh fruit (pitted cherries, raspberries, strawberries, chopped peaches, chopped plums, etc.) with ⅓ to ½ cup sugar until the mixture is thick and syrupy. Spoon the mixture onto a plate and run your finger through the liquid; the line made by your finger should hold its shape.

Raised Nut Crescents

Makes about 4 dozen cookies

2 cups unbleached all-purpose flour
¼ teaspoon salt
1 teaspoon baking powder
½ cup (1 stick) butter
1 package (2 teaspoons) active dry yeast
2 tablespoons warm (95°) water

2 eggs, separated
¼ cup sour cream
2 ounces pecans, ground fine
½ cup sugar
½ teaspoon Frangelico or Amaretto liqueur
Powdered sugar for dusting

Preheat the oven to 400°. Combine the flour, salt, and baking powder in a large bowl. Cut in the butter with your fingers, a pastry cutter, or 2 knives, until the mixture resembles coarse meal.

In a medium bowl, dissolve the yeast in the warm water. Beat in the egg yolks and sour cream; blend into the flour. Chill the dough for 1 hour. Grind the pecans in a blender, food processor, or nut grinder. Set aside. Beat the egg whites and sugar until stiff; add the ground pecans and liqueur. On a lightly floured board, divide the dough into 4 parts. Roll each part into a 10-inch circle. Cut each circle into 12 wedges. Spread 1 heaping teaspoon meringue on each wedge and carefully roll the large end of each wedge towards the point. Press the rolls together lightly and bend each into a crescent shape.

Bake on lightly greased baking sheets in the preheated oven for 10 to 12 minutes, or until lightly browned. Cool on wire racks and dust with powdered sugar.

BASIC TECHNIQUES

Correct skills with kitchen knives are essential not only for the finished, polished appearance of a dish but also for the correct cooking times of meats, vegetables, and fish: food not cut uniformly will not cook uniformly. Remember to keep your knives very sharp and to work carefully, cleanly, and with organization. Cutting your ingredients precisely will set the tone for the entire preparation of the dish.

Julienne

The definition of *julienne* is matchstick size: 1¼ inches long, ⅛ inch wide. Julienne strips may be longer—long strips of vegetables are very attractive as a garnish—and finer, as in fine julienne, which is 1/16 inch wide. The important point to consider is what the food to be cut will be used for. If for soup, food should be cut no longer than will fit inside a soup spoon. The way food is cut should also blend with the rest of the dish: 3-inch-long pieces of celery would not look right in a salad of potatoes cut into ½-inch dice.

First trim the vegetable to be cut into a uniform size by squaring up all 4 sides. From this squared piece, cut uniform slices about ⅛ inch thick. Stack these slices 3 thick and cut into uniform strips ⅛ inch wide. Fine julienne is prepared by the same procedure; simply cut the strips thinner. If desired, the strips may be shredded as fine as possible, which also makes an attractive garnish.

Dicing

Fine dice, mince, or *brunoise* is a 1/16-inch-square cut for vegetables to be used as a condiment, such as red or white onions with smoked salmon or caviar; and ingredients for consommé, fine forcemeats for stuffings or sausages; or in preparations in which the ingredient is intended to have a delicate, subtle effect. Small dice, ⅛ inch square, and medium dice, 3/16 inch square, are used when the color, flavor, and texture of the food are meant to be more pronounced. Large dice, ⅜ inch square, is used when the ingredient will be a major part of the dish, as in squash for chutney.

To dice, trim the ingredient evenly on all sides. Cut in 1/16-inch slices for fine dice, ⅛ inch slices for small dice, and so on. Stack the slices in strips of equal width. Line up the strips uniformly, and cut into equal-sized squares.

Slicing

Slicing is an important part of the presentation of meats, fish, poultry, and game as well as pâtés and terrines. A thin-bladed slicer with either a straight or scalloped edge is essential, and it must be razor sharp. Use a steel to keep the blade at its optimum sharpness. A dull knife or any knife other than a slicer will tear and rip, causing an unattractive appearance.

When slicing, always steady the food to be sliced with your free hand. Also be sure to pay close attention that the knife is kept at the same width at the end of the cut as in the beginning, to ensure that all the slices are uniform.

To slice on the bias, hold the knife at a 30- to 45-degree angle, depending on the slice you wish. This is an attractive cut for roast meats and poultry, and an excellent way to slice fish for even portions.

Boning and Filleting

Many people are unnecessarily frightened of boning meats and poultry and filleting fish. These techniques require only an understanding of simple anatomy, sharp knives, and a work surface that is large enough for the item being boned or filleted. The following instructions will enable you to prepare any of the meats, poultry, or fish in this book, and with a little practice you can become proficient and advance on to larger cuts if desired.

A medium-sized 7-inch to 9-inch flexible-bladed boning knife is the best choice for an all-purpose boning knife. A curved slicer, or scimitar, with a 10-inch to 12-inch blade is good for filleting large salmon or halibut.

Filleting Fish

Pacific fish may be divided into two categories: bottom fish, or flat fish, such as halibut and all types of sole; and upper-depth fish, or round fish, such as salmon, snapper, bass, etc.

Bottom fish have a central skeleton with two fillets on either side, top and bottom, and a thin cavity of body organs. The skeletal structure of upper-depth fish is wider and more cylinder-shaped, with two thicker fillets, one on each side of the central spine.

To fillet a bottom fish   Lay the fish securely on a dry cutting board so that it will not slide. Run your knife down the center of the fish along the bone, as shown in the photograph, to expose the center of the spine. With the tip of the knife, open the flesh away from the spine about ¼ inch on one side of the fish, all along its length. With the tip of the knife carefully placed right against the bone, run the knife the full length of the fish another ¼ inch in an even, smooth stroke. You should now have a ½-inch-thick slice cut away from the bone. Holding your knife flat against the bone again with your palm up, run the blade of the knife down the length of the fish, holding your opposite hand in the upper left-hand corner to steady the fish. Carefully fold the fillet over (with both hands if the fish is large) and cut the fillet away from the bottom of the rib cage along the full length. Repeat the process on the other side of the top of the fish for the second fillet. Turn the fish over and repeat the process for the third and fourth fillets. Reserve the bones for stock.

To remove the skin, lay the fillet on the work surface, flesh-side up. With a 10-inch French knife or slicer, cut through the flesh but not the skin ¼ inch from the tail end of the fillet. Hold the knife at a 30-degree angle, firmly grasp the ¼ inch of flesh and skin at the tail with one hand, and, in a smooth, even movement, run the blade of the knife along the full length of the fillet between the skin and flesh, holding the skin as tightly as possible.

To fillet salmon and other upper-depth swimmers   Lay the fish flat on the cutting board with the head toward your cutting hand and the body cavity facing away from you. Using a 10-inch French knife or fillet knife, cut through the flesh right behind the head and in a curve around the shape of the head to the spine. With the tip of the knife, carefully cut a ¼-inch slice of flesh away from the bone at the spine where it joins the head. Run the tip of the knife the full length of the spine, ¼ inch deep. Return your knife to the incision at the head, hold the knife firmly against the spine, and, in a smooth motion, insert the knife through the width of the fish flat on the spine. Holding the head of the fish firmly with your other hand, run the blade of the knife in a smooth, even motion—always keeping the knife flat against the spine—the length of the fish and through the skin just before the tail. Carefully lay the fillet over, skin-side down on the work surface, and trim it from the skeleton at the stomach wall.

With the butt of the knife, cut through the spine but not the flesh, at the tail. Insert the knife under the bone at this point. Hold the tail firmly in the other hand. Hold the knife completely flat on the flesh right under the spine. In a smooth, even motion, always keeping the knife absolutely flat, run the blade of the knife the full length of the fish to the head. Cut through the fillet at this point and lift the skeleton and head. With the tip of the knife, trim the small amount of bone from the upper part of the fillet and the rib cage in the upper corner. Trim off ½ to ¾ inch of the belly. Bones running down the center of the fillet at the thickest part are easiest removed with a needlenose pliers or tweezers. Remove the skin as described on page 148.

Boning Chicken and Game Birds

Many dishes are prepared from boneless chicken breasts, and their ease of preparation by sautéing or grilling makes this an ideal cut. As a rule, however, the flavor of chicken and game birds is greatly enhanced if they are cooked whole, allowed to rest so that their juices settle, then boned just before being served: the meat is more flavorful and juicy. The procedures for boning in the raw or cooked state are exactly the same and are not at all difficult.

To bone a chicken   Remove the giblets and neck from the body cavity, and place the chicken with the body cavity facing you.

Holding the drumstick in one hand and a sharp boning knife in the other, make an incision in the skin between the body and the leg to expose the leg joint. Firmly twist the leg flat against the cutting surface while holding the knife on the spot where the joint rotates. Cut through the joint at this spot, and sever the thigh from the body. Repeat the process on the other side. Holding the drumstick in one hand, move it slightly to show the joint. Cut through the joint with the butt of the knife to separate the drumstick from thigh. Repeat with the other drumstick. Trim the wings from the chicken at their base against the breast. Rotate the breast so that the neck opening faces your left, if you are right-handed. Run the tip of your knife lengthwise down the center of the breast, making 2 slices, one on either side of the breastbone. Insert your knife in the cut and, with smooth, even strokes, run the blade of the knife along the rib bones to lift the meat off the bone.

To bone the breast in one piece   This makes a cut called a *suprême*. Hold the chicken vertically by the tip of the breast. With a cleaver or the butt of a French knife, cut the breast away from the backbone with firm, even strokes, ending at the wing joint. Turn the breast bone-side up on the table and carefully notch the center of the breast cavity with the knife without cutting through the flesh. Carefully pull back the rib cage on either side of the incision and remove the breastbone.

The procedure for *boning game birds* is the same; the only difference is in the size of the birds. Duck, pheasant, partridge, grouse, and larger game birds are boned in the same fashion. Quail and squab are treated exactly the same, but the latter usually require only a sharp paring knife.

Remember to save all bones for stock. The bones of roasted birds have a particularly good flavor in sauces and soups.

Sautéing

This is the most widely used procedure in contemporary cooking and one that is essential to master. Remember the basics: Sautéing is done in a small amount of fat, without moisture, and over relatively high heat.

Choose heavy, flat-bottomed pans. The traditional classic cast-iron skillet is and probably always will be the premier pan for sautéing. It is heavy, it heats evenly, and it is easy to care for. Nonstick pans are also excellent, as they require little or no fat to sauté foods.

Make sure the food to be sautéed is evenly portioned for thickness and size, is dry, and is seasoned on both sides. If the food is breaded be sure that the breading mixture is light and even, not matted and wet.

If sautéing any food thicker than ¼ inch, preheat the oven to 375°. Sauté the item quickly on each side, then transfer the food to the oven. The heat exposure to all sides of the sautéed item will cook it evenly and quickly. Remove the pan from the oven with the ingredient just underdone, and finish it on the burner.

Heat the butter or oil in the pan, then add the food to be sautéed. Allow the food to brown evenly before turning, and use tongs, not a fork, to avoid puncturing the food and allowing its juices to run out. Do not overcrowd the pan. Cook in small batches, preferably keeping the sautéed foods warm while you prepare the next batch. Crowding the pan will lower the heat, causing the food to steam, thus becoming soggy and tough. Meats, fish, and poultry are done when they are firm and springy to the touch. Remember they will continue to cook when removed from the pan and while being kept warm before serving, which often is up to 3 to 4 minutes, so remove them from the pan slightly underdone.

Most vegetables should be blanched by being boiled briefly in salted water, immersed in ice water, and well drained prior to being sautéed. The vegetables will cook more evenly when they are blanched and quickly sautéed just before serving. This also enables the cook to control the timing of the dish to the second, which is of utmost importance in the final moments of preparation.

Follow the same procedure as with all sautéing. Heat the oil or butter in the pan and add the vegetables, season, and toss or stir lightly. Just when the vegetables are nearly done, swirl a small amount of softened butter into the vegetable juices to coat them.

Steaming

Asian cooks have used steaming for centuries, in part because it is an economical method of preparation using relatively low heat and also because of the delicate magic it imparts to food. You do not need a bamboo steamer, although they are wonderful to cook in. A wire rack set in a covered pot over simmering liquid is quite adequate.

The wonderful aspect of steaming is that you can use flavored steaming liquids to enhance meats, fish, and poultry (see Steamed Duck with Chanterelles, page 87). Allow the mixture to simmer for 10 to 15 minutes to develop its flavors. The mixture could be a simple court bouillon, an herbal-wine infusion, a vinegar-based stock, or a soy-rice wine mixture. The list of ingredients and their combinations is endless. Seaweed immersed in white wine is an excellent method for steaming fish, for example.

Remember to season the meat, fish, or poultry well. Herbs laid over or stuffed inside of steamed foods add an intriguing taste. Be sure the food does not touch the liquid and that there is plenty of room for the circulation of steam above and around the food. Keep the heat low and check the level of the liquid to keep it replenished, if necessary, with additional boiling liquid.

Steaming without a rack in a small amount of liquid is also a wonderful technique and is preferable for many foods. Use a pan that is just the right size to hold the items snugly; a pan that is too small will cause uneven cooking, and one that is too large will cause flavor to dissipate. Add the food to be steamed to the pan, and add a small amount of liquid such as wine, stock, vinegar, or soy sauce—just enough to cover the bottom of the pan. Bring the liquid to a boil, dot the items being steamed with a small amount of butter, season lightly, and cover the pan tightly. Lower the heat to medium. Toss the pan lightly to insure even cooking. Check for doneness and, when about three-fourths cooked, remove the lid. Raise the heat to high and toss the steamed food in its own juices until the food absorbs the liquid and is shiny. This technique is excellent for vegetables, fish, shellfish, and poultry.

Grilling

Grilling has experienced a renaissance in the past few years, to say the least. And well it should, for it is the perfect way to prepare many dishes. Grilling must be done precisely and with great care and attention, however. An overcooked dish from the grill is a waste. But by using certain easy and basic techniques, you can be assured of enjoying the pleasures of juicy, fragrant, and tasty dishes from the fire.

In preparing the fire, the choice of wood or charcoal is discretionary. The taste of alder or fruit woods such as apple, cherry, or plum is most preferable, followed by hickory or oak. I find that mesquite is too sharp and acrid a taste and overwhelms grilled foods. Many, however, swear by it, so if you enjoy it, by all means use it. With any wood, prepare the fire and allow the coals to burn down to medium-hot, the point at which they are white, but still glistening with red.

Be sure to have the meat to be grilled at room temperature, dry, lightly brushed with oil, and seasoned on all sides. Clean the grill grates well, oil them lightly, and be sure that they are very hot.

Lay the food on the grill over the hottest area of coals. Sear the food well, being careful to extinguish any flare-ups with a small amount of water (a water pistol or a spray bottle is perfect for this). When the food is evenly browned, not black, turn it and sear over the hottest coals. When well seared on both sides, move the food to the side of the grill. Allow it to cook slowly by the reflected heat of the coals, until done. Baste lightly, if you wish, with melted butter or flavored oils. Don't overdo this; if properly cooked, the grilled meat, fish, or poultry will have its own natural juices. Over-basting will result in a soggy dish and flare-ups from the fire.

When about three-fourths done, move the grilled food back to the center of the fire to finish grilling for a few minutes. Handle food carefully when removing it from the grill. Allow meat and poultry to rest for 5 to 8 minutes before slicing or serving.

Firm-fleshed fish such as halibut, salmon, or swordfish are the best for grilling, as are shrimp, scallops, and oysters, which do well on skewers. For a real treat, grill shellfish in their shells and serve them right off the grill. All types of cod as well as sole are also very nice on the grill, but the fish must be absolutely fresh, the grill very clean, and the fire hot enough that they can be grilled on one side, then turned and removed.

Roasting

There is nothing that can compare to the flavor of a perfectly roasted piece of meat, poultry, game, or fish. This is the simplest of cooking procedures; to do it well requires skill and a watchful eye.

Always have the food to be roasted at room temperature. For larger roasts this will mean 1 to 2 hours at room temperature, and less time for smaller roasts. The fundamental principle is that if the entire piece is at the same temperature, as opposed to being warm on the outside and cold in the center, it will cook evenly, and in less time.

Sear all roasted items well in the pan before placing in the oven. For *larger* pieces, such as whole turkeys, large roasts, or geese, sear in a preheated oven at 475° for the first 20 minutes of cooking time.

After searing, larger pieces should be roasted at a low temperature, preferably 275°, to ensure the least amount of shrinkage and loss of juices. Raise the heat to 475° for the final 10 to 15 minutes.

Season meats well, making sure to season the body cavities of poultry or game birds, as well as the outside skin. It is preferable to roast food in the same pan in which it has been seared, in order to capture all the natural juices and to insure even cooking.

As a rule of thumb, it is best to first sear all *smaller* roasts— such as lamb or veal loin, beef tenderloin, boneless roasts, game birds, venison, and elk—on the top of the stove, then to roast them in a very hot oven (475°) for a period of about 10 to 12 minutes. Then, open the door, reduce the heat, and allow the oven to cool to 250°, turn the roast, and allow it to finish at this temperature until it reaches the desired doneness. The hot juices seared into the meat will penetrate to the center, cooking the meat from within as well as from the outside. Cooking it first at a high temperature followed by a lower temperature allows the meat to cook evenly, without excess shrinkage.

Always allow roasted meats to rest 5 to 10 minutes before carving or slicing to allow the juices to settle in the meat.

Smoking and Curing

The smoking and curing of foods is perhaps the most singular traditional cooking technique in Northwest cuisine, for it is an art that was handed down to us and is still practiced by the Native Americans. Their culture has always centered around the salmon, with much of their mythology and ritual based on the fish's yearly runs. The principles of curing and smoking in this chapter are based on traditional Indian methods, the only difference being that our present aim is primarily to enhance flavor rather than to preserve the fish.

The procedures and techniques of smoking and curing offer the opportunity to experiment and develop your own "custom smoke," and the fantastic aroma of sweet wood smoke, mingled with the fragrance of sturgeon, trout, pheasant, or quail will linger in your memory. I will always remember the look on the face of an old Indian man who was smoking fish on the Washington Coast near Neah Bay. When I asked him what he was doing, he replied, "Just makin' smoke." I understand his contentment.

Curing is divided into two categories—brine and dry cure—and three grades: mild, medium, and hard. We will use mild cure in both brine and dry. After curing it is essential to air-dry all smoked food, which firms it and creates a smooth texture. A household fan blowing over cured food works very well, as does refrigerating the food overnight uncovered, or wind-drying it outdoors, the most traditional method.

Brine Cure

Makes enough to cure 4 whole trout,
2 whole pheasants, or 6 duck breasts

1/4 *cup pickling salt*
3 *tablespoons sugar*
2 *quarts cold water*

2 *bay leaves*
2 *thyme sprigs*
2 *parsley sprigs*
2 *garlic cloves, crushed*

Dissolve the salt and sugar in the water and add the herbs and garlic. Wash the food to be smoked well and immerse it in the brine, weighing it down with an inverted plate if necessary. Cure for 4 to 6 hours in the refrigerator. Remove from the brine, drain, and air-dry for 2 hours with a household fan blowing air over the food. Smoke with cold smoke as described below.

Dry Cure

Makes enough to cure 2 pounds of fish

This cure is recommended for firm, white-fleshed fish such as halibut, sturgeon, bass, and salmon. It is not recommended for poultry or game birds.

3 *tablespoons pickling salt*
2 *tablespoons sugar*
2 *parsley sprigs, chopped*
½ *teaspoon chopped fresh thyme*

Place the fish in a stainless steel or glass container. Combine all the ingredients and sprinkle over the fish, lightly rubbing the mixture into the flesh on both sides. Cover tightly with plastic wrap and refrigerate for 8 hours or overnight.

Drain the fish and leave it uncovered for 4 hours or overnight in the refrigerator. Air-dry for 2 hours at room temperature with a household fan blowing air over the fish. Smoke the fish with cold smoke as described below.

Note   The fish may also be placed on cooling racks and air-dried outdoors on dry windy days.

Cold Smoking

The grade of smoke—mild, medium, or hard—depends on the temperature reached in the smoker during the smoking process. The recipes in this book use the cold smoke process, in which the temperature never goes above 90°. A standard oven thermometer placed inside the smoker is the most accurate method for maintaining the temperature.

There are many good home-model smokers available in gourmet cookware stores and sporting goods stores. A conventional kettle grill with a cover also works very well.

Electric-powered smokers are the most easily controlled. Wood chips are placed in a pan set over the hot coils. For convenience and consistency, the commercial home apparatus is recommended. You may, however, build a small fire in a portable barbecue with hardwood briquettes and cover the coals with hardwood shavings or chips that have been soaked in water. Be careful the fire doesn't flare up. The important thing to remember is to control the temperature inside the smoker carefully and to allow the cured food to smoke gently. The food should have a delicate wood-smoked taste and above all should retain its moisture, texture, and flavor. Remember, too, that the flavor of smoke will become more pronounced as the food is cooled.

The following times are recommended:

Trout, whole: *20 minutes*
Fish fillets (halibut, bass, etc.): *15 minutes*
Salmon fillets: *30 minutes*
Pheasant and duck, whole: *4 to 6 hours*
Quail: *1½ hours*
Duck breasts: *1 hour*

Be sure to cool the finished smoked food as soon as possible. Brush it with peanut oil and wrap in plastic wrap. Mild-cured smoked fish will be at its best for 1 to 2 days after smoking, while game birds, boned or whole, are best eaten within 3 to 4 days.

Smoked Vegetables

A variety of vegetables may be smoked to be used as a flavoring in sauces (such as Smoked Tomato Coulis, page 47); as a flavoring for dips or dressings; smoked and served chilled as part of an appetizer or antipasto; or as a garnish (Smoked Trout with Walla Walla Onions, page 52). If using vegetables whole it is usually best to blanch them first, then immerse them in ice water, drain, and dry before smoking. If using vegetables as a base for a sauce, it is advisable to blanch them, immerse them in ice water, drain, and press out excess liquid by squeezing them lightly in cheesecloth or a kitchen towel.

Season the vegetables well and smoke them with cold smoke for 15 to 25 minutes, either on skewers or wire cooling racks to allow the smoke to circulate.

A wide range of vegetables adapt well to smoking, especially squash, eggplant, corn, tomatoes, peppers, onions, and leeks. Let your imagination be your guide and experiment with different combinations, such as smoked leeks in a citrus vinaigrette, smoked eggplant dip for vegetables, smoked bell peppers pureed for a soup or sauce, and smoked shallots as a garnish for beef or game. Remember that the smoked flavor should be subtle, not overpowering, both in the smoked food and in the dish in which it is used.

BASIC RECIPES

Stocks and sauces serve a twofold purpose in all fine cooking: They complement and enhance the flavor of soups, meats, poultry, fish, game, and vegetables; and they form the foundation of the true flavor of each dish. The stocks in this chapter are concentrated essences. The sauces are made of these essences in combination with ingredients that will enliven their flavors. A properly prepared fish stock, for example, begins with a full-flavored, aromatic broth to be used as a basis for a rich chowder, fish stew, or soup. Adding shallots, mushrooms, white wine, and cream to the fish stock creates a creamy, rich basic sauce that can be varied to form an endless array of sauces. Stock can be kept in the refrigerator for 3 days. It freezes well and is most conveniently frozen in 2-quart containers.

Stocks and sauces bring all the components of a dish into clear focus. Prepare them carefully, and treat them as liquid gold, savoring every drop. In each drop is the essence of fine cooking.

Fish Stock

Makes about 3 pints

5½ pounds fish bones (halibut, cod, sole, haddock, snapper, etc.)
1 medium leek
2 celery stalks
1 medium onion
2 bay leaves
2 thyme sprigs
4 to 5 shallots
2 garlic cloves
1 cup mushrooms and/or mushroom stems, chopped

12 peppercorns, crushed
2 cloves
1 cup dry white wine
5 cups water

Chop the bones into small pieces with a cleaver; wash the bones well. Combine all the remaining ingredients, except the water, in an large, heavy pot and bring to a simmer over low heat, stirring gently. Cover the pot and steam the ingredients for 5 minutes. Add the water. Simmer the stock for 20 minutes, skimming any impurities off the top. Remove from the heat, allow to sit for 5 minutes, and strain through a fine sieve.

Brown Veal Stock

Makes about 2 quarts

5 pounds veal shin bones, chopped into small pieces
2 pounds veal shanks
4 tablespoons peanut oil
About 1 gallon water
3 unpeeled onions, chopped
3 carrots, chopped
4 celery stalks, chopped
4 garlic cloves
2 bay leaves
6 thyme sprigs
20 peppercorns, crushed

Preheat the oven to 400°. Rub the bones and veal shanks lightly with 2 tablespoons of the peanut oil. Roast in a roasting pan or on a baking sheet in the preheated oven for 35 to 40 minutes, or until the bones and meat are a deep mahogany brown color. Place the bones and meat in a stockpot, scraping all the bits on the bottom of the roasting pan into the pot. Add the water, covering the bones and meat by 2 inches. Bring to a simmer over low heat, skimming any impurities off the top. Simmer for 4 hours.

Sauté all the remaining ingredients in the remaining 2 tablespoons peanut oil in a large, heavy skillet, or roast in a 400° oven, until evenly browned. Add to the stock and simmer for 3 to 4 more hours, skimming. The stock may be simmered longer if desired, up to 12 hours. Strain through a coarse sieve, then through a fine sieve, and let cool to room temperature. Skim any excess fat off the top of the stock and refrigerate.

Lamb Stock

Follow the recipe for Brown Veal Stock, above, using lamb bones and simmering the stock for a total of 8 hours.

Chicken Stock

Makes about 2 quarts

5 to 6 chicken carcasses (about 4 pounds)
2 onions
2 carrots
3 celery stalks
3 parsley sprigs
1 leek
4 thyme sprigs
3 bay leaves
2 garlic cloves
12 peppercorns, crushed

Chop the chicken carcasses into small pieces with a cleaver; wash well. Place in a heavy 1½- to 2-gallon stockpot and cover with cold water. Bring to a simmer over low heat, skimming any impurities off the top. Chop the vegetables coarsely and add to the stock along with the herbs, garlic, and peppercorns.

Simmer for 2½ hours, skimming occasionally, and strain. Cool to room temperature, and remove any excess fat from the surface. The stock will keep for 2 to 3 days refrigerated, and is best if frozen no longer than 2 weeks.

Game Stock

Makes about 2 quarts

12 to 18 quail carcasses; 2 pheasant carcasses; 2 duck
    carcasses; or 3 pounds venison or elk bones
2 tablespoons peanut oil
1 unpeeled onion, chopped
2 celery stalks, chopped
1 carrot, chopped
4 garlic cloves
1 teaspoon juniper berries, crushed
4 whole cloves
3 bay leaves
2 parsley sprigs
2 thyme sprigs
2 cups water

Chop the carcasses or bones into small pieces. In a heavy 1½- to 2-gallon stockpot, sauté the carcasses or bones in the peanut oil over medium heat until evenly browned, stirring often; or roast the bones in a preheated 400° oven for about 35 minutes. Add the vegetables and garlic and sauté over medium heat until well browned; do not burn. Add the juniper berries, cloves, herbs, and the 2 cups water. Scrape up any browned bits on the bottom of the pan and reduce over high heat to a glaze.

Add enough water to cover the bones and bring slowly to a simmer, skimming often, and cook 2½ hours for game bird carcasses and up to 8 hours for venison or elk bones. Strain through a coarse strainer, then a fine sieve, let cool, and skim any excess fat off the surface. Refrigerate for up to 3 days, or freeze for up to 1 month.

Venison Stock

Makes about 6½ cups stock

5 pounds venison bones
2 tablespoons peanut oil
1 cup Cabernet Sauvignon or other full-bodied red wine
2 carrots, chopped
1 onion, chopped
2 celery stalks, chopped
2 thyme sprigs
2 parsley sprigs
2 bay leaves
2 cloves

Preheat the oven to 400°. Crack the venison bones as small as possible with a cleaver and brush with 1 tablespoon of the peanut oil. Roast the bones in the preheated oven in a heatproof skillet until they are a dark mahogany brown. Remove from the skillet to a 6- to 8-quart stockpot. Add the wine to the skillet, bring to a boil, and scrape up any brown bits adhering to the pan. Add this to the bones in the pot and add water to cover the bones by 1 inch. Slowly bring the water to a simmer.

While the stock is heating, sauté the vegetables in the remaining 1 tablespoon peanut oil until browned. Skim the surface foam off the stock as it comes to the simmer and add the browned vegetables and herbs. Simmer 6 to 8 hours and strain, removing any fat from the surface. The stock can be prepared 2 days in advance and refrigerated. The stock may also be frozen.

Natural Juices

Makes 1 pint

A natural juice is prepared from beef, veal, lamb, pork, fowl, or game and is a highly concentrated essence of flavor. The preparation requires both time and meticulous attention; the results are exquisite. The essential technique is the repeated rapid reduction of liquid over high heat to extract all the flavors from the ingredients. The following basic method and proportions may be used for any natural meat juices. Natural juices may be stored in the refrigerator tightly covered and are best used within 3 to 4 days. They may also be frozen for up to 1 month.

1 to 2 pounds bones or carcasses, cut in ½-inch to 1-inch
*   pieces*
1 tablespoon peanut oil
2 to 3 shallots, chopped
¼ cup chopped mushrooms
½ medium onion, chopped
½ celery stalk, chopped
½ medium carrot, chopped
1 bay leaf
1 thyme sprig
1 garlic clove, chopped
½ teaspoon black peppercorns, crushed
8 cups veal, chicken, game, lamb, or other stock (see pages
*   157–159), or canned chicken broth*

Chop the bones or carcasses into the smallest possible pieces with a cleaver or the butt of a French knife. It is essential that the pieces be chopped small, to allow for the maximum extraction of juices.

Heat a heavy 4- to 6-quart saucepan over high heat until it begins to smoke; add the oil and the bones or carcasses. Brown well on all sides, stirring rapidly. Continue to stir over high heat until the carcasses or bones are evenly browned. Add the vegetables, herbs, and peppercorns. Lower the heat to medium and, stirring occasionally, sauté until well browned. Return the heat to high and continue stirring, scraping any bits off the bottom of the pan.

When the bones and vegetables are completely browned, add approximately 2 cups of the stock to barely cover the ingredients. Bring to a boil and continue to boil rapidly over high heat until the liquid is reduced to about ¼ cup. Stir well to keep any ingredients from sticking to the bottom and add another 2 cups of the stock. Return to a boil and repeat the procedure, reducing to approximately ¼ cup.

The reduction will now be very thick, syrupy, and shiny. Add another 2 cups of the stock and again reduce to about 1 cup over high heat, stirring occasionally.

Add the remaining 2 cups of stock. Bring to a boil and lower the heat to medium. Skim any impurities off the sauce. Continue to simmer, skimming, for approximately 30 minutes, or until the juice is clear and the flavor is concentrated. Strain the natural juice through a coarse sieve, then a fine sieve, pressing all the liquids from the bones and vegetables. Skim any impurities from the surface.

Note   You can save the bones from game birds, lamb, chickens, etc., and freeze them until you have enough to proceed with this recipe. Or, if quantities of bones are available, increase the proportions of the recipe and freeze the natural juice in small amounts.

Vegetable Stock

Makes 4 cups

This stock is an excellent base for soups, for braising vegetables, and for use in light sauces. Other vegetables may be added but some, like broccoli, cauliflower, green beans, or turnips, will impart too much of their own flavor to the stock.

4 to 5 shallots
1 onion
3 celery stalks
3 carrots
1 leek
2 parsley sprigs
2 thyme sprigs
2 bay leaves
2 garlic cloves
½ cup mushrooms
2 tablespoons peanut oil

Chop all the vegetables, herbs, garlic, and mushrooms coarsely, and sauté them in the peanut oil in a heavy saucepan over low heat until the onion is translucent. Add water to cover and bring to a boil. Simmer for 20 minutes and strain through a fine sieve. Refrigerate for up to 2 days or freeze.

Crayfish Sauce

Makes about 2 cups

This sauce is excellent served with almost any white fish such as halibut, cod, or sole, and is equally delicious prepared with crab shells. It is also wonderful with pasta or ravioli, and, if thinned with 1 to 1½ cups fish stock, makes a rich, luxurious soup.

2 tablespoons peanut oil
2 pounds live or cooked crayfish
1½ cups dry white wine
1 carrot, chopped
1 medium onion, chopped
2 celery stalks
1 leek, chopped
8 to 10 mushrooms, chopped

4 shallots, chopped
2 garlic cloves
2 thyme sprigs
2 tarragon sprigs
½ cup brandy
3 cups Fish Stock, page 157, or bottled clam juice
3 tomatoes, chopped
1 teaspoon tomato paste
2 bay leaves
1 teaspoon Beurre Manie, page 165
1 cup heavy cream

Heat 1 tablespoon of the peanut oil in a heavy, medium sauce-pan. If using live crayfish, add them all at once to the pan with ¾ cup of the white wine, stir rapidly, and cover the pot. Steam for 2 minutes. Remove the crayfish from the pot and allow to cool enough to handle. Pull the tail meat from the body section, peel the tail, and reserve the tail meat for another use (such as Crayfish and Spot Prawn Minestrone with Dungeness Crab Ravioli, page 49); reserve the shells and heads for the sauce. If using precooked shells, remove the meat from the tails and proceed with the next step.

Meanwhile, in a large saucepan, sauté the vegetables, mushrooms, shallots, garlic, and herbs in the remaining 1 tablespoon peanut oil over low heat until translucent. Raise the heat to high and add the crayfish heads and reserved shells from tails. Sauté over high heat for 2 minutes, stirring often and crushing the shells with the spoon. Add the brandy and reduce by two thirds. Add the remaining ¾ cup of wine and reduce by half. Add the fish stock, tomatoes, tomato paste, and bay leaves and bring to a boil. Lower the heat and simmer the sauce for 35 minutes.

Prepare the *beurre manie*. Strain the sauce, reserving the shells in the saucepan. Crush the shells well with the back of the spoon or a meat tenderizer into a complete pulp. Return the stock to the shells, bring to the boil again, and whip in the *beurre manie*. Simmer the sauce for 20 minutes. Add the cream, return the sauce to a boil and simmer for 10 minutes.

Strain the sauce through a fine sieve or cheesecloth, pressing out all liquid. Puree on high speed in a blender or food processor until completely smooth. Adjust the seasoning. If the sauce should become grainy or break, simply return it to blender and blend until smooth.

White Butter Sauce

Makes ½ cup

This sauce is best when used within 1 hour.

1 teaspoon peanut oil
2 shallots, chopped
4 mushrooms, chopped
1 thyme sprig
1 parsley sprig
2 tablespoons white wine vinegar
2 tablespoons heavy cream
½ cup (1 stick) cold unsalted butter, cut into pieces

In a medium saucepan, heat the oil and sauté the shallots, mushrooms, thyme, and parsley until translucent. Add the vinegar and reduce until evaporated. Add the cream and reduce until lightly thickened. Remove the pan from the heat and whisk in the butter a piece at a time, making sure the sauce remains creamy. Strain through a fine sieve, pressing out all the liquids; set aside and keep warm.

Note Refrigerate any leftover sauce. To reuse, in a heavy, medium pan, reduce 2 tablespoons heavy cream until thick, then remove from the heat and whisk spoonfuls of the cold sauce into the cream.

Red Butter Sauce

Makes ½ cup

1 teaspoon peanut oil
2 shallots, chopped
4 mushrooms, chopped
1 parsley sprig
1 thyme sprig
3 tablespoons red wine vinegar
½ cup red wine
2 tablespoons heavy cream
½ cup (1 stick) cold unsalted butter, cut into pieces

In a medium saucepan, heat the oil and sauté the shallots, mushrooms, parsley, and thyme over medium heat until the shallots are translucent. Add the vinegar and reduce until almost evaporated. Add the red wine and reduce to ¼ cup. Add the cream and reduce until thickened. Remove from the heat and whisk in the butter, piece by piece, making sure the sauce remains creamy. Keep warm until ready to use.

Vin Blanc Sauce

Makes about 1 cup

This sauce is best used the same day it is made; it may be refrigerated for up to 2 days.

2 tablespoons butter
2 shallots, chopped
4 to 6 mushrooms, chopped
3 tablespoons chopped onion
1 thyme sprig
1 parsley sprig

2 bay leaves
1 cup dry white wine
1 cup Fish Stock, page 157, or bottled clam juice
1 cup heavy cream

Melt the butter in a heavy saucepan over low heat and sauté the shallots, mushrooms, onion, and herbs until the shallots and onion are translucent. Add ¼ cup of the wine and reduce over high heat until almost evaporated. Add the remaining ¾ cup wine and reduce over high heat by half. Add the fish stock and reduce by half. Add the cream and simmer for 5 minutes, or until lightly thickened. Strain through a fine sieve, pressing out all the liquids.

Mignonette Sauce

Makes ⅓ cup, or enough for 18 to 24 oysters

This sauce is for serving with oysters on the half shell; it is excellent with all types of chilled seafood.

2 shallots, minced
1½ tablespoons black peppercorns
Red wine vinegar to cover

Place the shallots in a small container. Crush the peppercorns coarsely on the cutting board where the shallots were minced. Add to the shallots. Add the red wine vinegar just until the shallot-peppercorn mixture is covered. Allow to sit for 1 hour. Store in a tightly covered jar, refrigerated, for up to 2 days.

Mayonnaise

Makes 1½ cups

This basic sauce is the foundation of an endless number of cold sauces and is a classic accompaniment to cold meats, poultry, seafood, and vegetables. Herbs, mustards, aromatic stocks, horseradish, and fruit and vegetable purees are just a few of the many possible additions.

2 large egg yolks, at room temperature
½ teaspoon fresh lemon juice or more
1⅓ cups vegetable oil
½ teaspoon Dijon mustard
Salt and fresh-ground pepper to taste

In a large bowl, whisk the eggs yolks and lemon juice together until the yolks begin to thicken. Whisk in the oil very slowly until the mayonnaise thickens, then add the remaining oil in larger amounts while whisking. Add the Dijon mustard and season with salt, pepper, and extra lemon juice if you like.

Note   This mayonnise can also be made in a blender or food processor; pour in the oil in a very thin stream until the mixture thickens.

Mushroom Essence

Makes about ½ cup

Prepared with wild or domestic mushrooms, this reduction is a great enhancer of many soups and sauces and is especially delicious when added to a dish of wild mushrooms (see page 83). Chicken, veal, or game essence may be prepared in the same manner, omitting the wild mushrooms and reducing the stock over very low heat until thick and syrupy. The resulting essence is great for enriching sauces and soups. Use carefully; it is very potent. It will keep indefinitely in the refrigerator.

1 tablespoon peanut oil
2 shallots, minced
1 garlic clove, minced
2 thyme sprigs
2 to 3 cups mushrooms and/or mushroom trimmings, chopped
3 to 4 cups Chicken Stock (page 158), Veal Stock (page 157), or canned chicken broth

In a heavy saucepan or skillet, heat the oil and sauté the shallots, garlic, and thyme until browned. Add the mushrooms and/or trimmings and sauté over high heat, stirring often. Add ½ cup of the stock and reduce to 1 tablespoon. Repeat the process 3 more times, reducing the stock down until it becomes very syrupy, and stirring to avoid scorching. Add 1 cup stock and lower the heat to medium. Continue reducing to a glaze and adding stock until all the stock is used. Reduce, using low heat in the final stages to avoid scorching, until the liquid is clear and very concentrated. Strain through a fine sieve, pressing out all the liquids; cool and refrigerate.

Tomato Coulis

Makes about 2½ cups

This coulis is an excellent accompaniment to grilled fish, poultry, or veal and is also good with pasta. Chilled, it makes a fine sauce for poached fish, chilled vegetables, or seafood pâtés or terrines. It may also be used without cooking.

1 shallot, chopped
1½ pounds ripe tomatoes, peeled, seeded, and chopped
2 garlic cloves
2 tablespoons olive oil
Salt and pepper to taste

Combine the shallot, tomatoes, and garlic in a blender or food processor and blend on high speed for 10 seconds. Slowly add the olive oil. Bring this mixture to a boil in a heavy, medium saucepan and simmer for 30 seconds. Return to the blender or processor for 30 seconds. Adjust the seasoning.

Fruit Coulis

Makes 1¼ cups

A perfect accompaniment to ice cream, poached or stewed fruit, or a plate of assorted fresh fruit served with your favorite cookies. Pears, peaches, and nectarines should be peeled before pureeing, as their skins will darken the sauce. Add sugar according to the sweetness of the fruit. Berries in the height of summer will need only a tablespoon of sugar, if any at all.

8 or 9 ounces fresh fruit
⅓ cup sugar, or to taste

Peel, pit, hull, or stem the fruit as necessary; cut large fruit into chunks. Combine the fruit and sugar in a blender or food processor and blend on medium speed for 5 minutes, or until well blended. Berries such as raspberries, blackberries, and loganberries then should be strained through a fine sieve to remove seeds.

Spoon Cheese

Makes about 3 cups

This fresh cheese is delicious with fruits or raw vegetables for a light lunch or appetizer, as an addition to a cheese assortment, or with fresh fruit. It is also excellent as a substitute for cream in sauces and soups.

1 pound whole-milk ricotta
5 tablespoons plain yogurt
Pinch salt

Purchase the freshest ricotta possible. Place the ricotta and the yogurt in a blender or a food processor and process on high speed until there is no trace of graininess. Add the salt. Strain through a fine sieve. Store the mixture, covered, for 12 hours or overnight. The cheese will culture and thicken.

Beurre Manie

Combine equal parts of softened butter and flour in a blender, food processor, a mixing bowl, or by hand. Prepare in small batches and use small amounts as needed to thicken soups.

Clarified Butter

Makes about ⅔ cup

I cup (2 sticks) butter

Melt the butter in a small saucepan over low heat, skimming all foam off the surface. Carefully pour off the clear yellow liquid, leaving the milk solids on the bottom. Use the milk solids in soups or sauces, and store the clarified butter in the refrigerator.

Basic Vinaigrette

Makes approximately ½ cup

The quality of vinaigrette is determined solely by the quality of the oil and vinegar used to make it. Any vinegar may be used: cider, red or white wine, balsamic, sherry, or any of the numerous herbal or fruit vinegars. When using sherry vinegar, adjust the strength with a small amount of red or white vinegar, as it is very potent.

Adding herbs to the vinegar and egg before the oil will create any number of herbal vinaigrettes. A few spinach leaves or parsley sprigs will also enhance the color. Be sure to taste as you go, as many herbs will intensify when they are blended. Whole-grain mustard, saffron, vegetables (such as beets, daikon radish sprouts, tomatoes), and fruits and berries also lend themselves well to vinaigrette preparations. Use your imagination, remembering that the vinaigrette is meant to enhance and brighten the taste of the main ingredient of the dish or salad.

1 egg white
2 tablespoons good-quality vinegar
6 tablespoons peanut, vegetable, or olive oil (if using nut oil
  other than peanut oil, use 2 tablespoons in combination
  with 3 tablespoons peanut or vegetable oil)
Salt and pepper to taste
Dash fresh lemon juice

Combine the egg white and vinegar in a blender, or whisk together in a mixing bowl. Add the oil in a drizzle until the mixture is emulsified. Season with salt, pepper, and lemon juice.

Herb Vinegars

Makes 1 quart

An herb-vinegar infusion is only as good as the vinegar you begin with. A medium-priced wine vinegar, naturally aged, is preferable to distilled vinegars from a supermarket shelf, which are usually watered down. Any type of herb may be used, as well as pesticide-free blossoms such as chive, borage, nasturtium, and arugula, to name a few. If you are picking herbs from your own garden, try to harvest them before they blossom, on a sunny afternoon when the herb oils are at their peak.

1 quart packed fresh herb sprigs or blossoms
1 quart good-quality white wine or red wine vinegar

Pack the herbs tightly into glass or ceramic containers. Cover with the vinegar. Store the vinegar, covered with cheesecloth, in a cool, dark place for a minimum of 1 month. At that time, the flavor of the herbs will have permeated the vinegar, and the resulting vinegar can be poured off into individual bottles along with some sprigs of the herb and covered. Or the vinegar may remain in the container to be used as needed.

A grayish, cloudy film may form on top of the vinegar during infusion. This is the "mother," a natural starter that should be left undisturbed. Before straining off any vinegar, remove the film with a spoon, then return it to the original infusion.

Additional seasonings such as garlic, chilies, cilantro, mustard seeds, coriander seeds, and peppercorns may be added with the herbs if desired. It is best to use small amounts of these strong seasonings, however, unless you want the specific taste of the seasoning to be central to the vinegar, as in a garlic-dill vinegar or jalapeño-sage vinegar.

Note   To prepare herb vinegar from wine, follow the same procedure as above, substituting dry white or red wine for the vinegar and adding a "mother," which can be purchased from winemaking supply shops. Eight ounces of commercial mother will convert 1 gallon of wine to vinegar. Allow the vinegar to age for a minimum of three months in a warm (75°) place.

Court Bouillon

Makes 2 quarts

This is a great flavor enhancer when used to poach fish, shellfish, or poultry. It can be varied according to your whim and the seasoning of the dish it is intended for.

2 quarts water
5 tablespoons herb or white wine vinegar
1 cup chopped leek
1 cup chopped onions
½ cup chopped celery
2 garlic cloves
6 parsley sprigs
2 bay leaves
1 tablespoon white peppercorns, crushed
4 fresh thyme sprigs
Salt to taste

Combine all the ingredients in a medium stockpot. Bring to a boil and simmer for 15 minutes. Strain through a fine sieve.

Basic Fresh Pickle

*Makes about 3½ cups, enough to flavor about 1 pound of
vegetables, fish, or shellfish*

This basic fresh pickle is used as an infusion to add flavor to
vegetables, not to preserve them. The liquid may be enhanced
with any number of herbs or spices such as dill, tarragon, basil,
chives, rosemary, marjoram, oregano, curry, mustard, coriander, turmeric, or cumin, to name a few. Basic Fresh Pickle may
also be used to pickle fish and shellfish.

1⅔ cups white wine vinegar
1⅔ cups water
1 teaspoon sugar
1 teaspoon salt
2 teaspoons mixed pickling spice
2 garlic cloves
3 thyme sprigs

In a non-aluminum saucepan, combine all the ingredients and
bring to a boil. Simmer for 5 minutes and allow to infuse until
cool. Strain if desired.

Wash about 1 pound of vegetables such as cucumbers, beans,
squashes, mushrooms, etc., then cut them into uniform pieces,
or if small, use whole. Pack the vegetables snugly in sterilized
jars, along with sprigs of fresh herbs or garlic cloves if desired.
Pour the cooled pickle over the vegetables, cover, and refrigerate overnight. The vegetables are then ready to eat and will
keep up to 2 weeks, refrigerated.

If using fish or shellfish, wash the fish or shellfish well, trim
into uniform pieces, and pack snugly in sterilized jars. Pour the
pickle over, cover, and refrigerate overnight. The pickled fish is
then ready to eat and is best eaten within 2 days.

Herb Oils

Makes 2 cups

Oils flavored with fresh herbs are the perfect flavor enhance-
ment for many foods, as they add both clarity of taste and lightness. Use only high-quality oils and store the herb oils in tightly
covered containers in a cool, dark place.

If you are gathering the herbs, do so on a sunny day, preferably when the herbs are near bloom. If purchasing the herbs,
choose the very freshest.

1½ cups fresh herbs (basil, sage, oregano, chives, tarragon,
thyme, summer savory, etc.), coarsely chopped
2 cups extra-virgin olive oil, peanut oil, or vegetable oil

Sterilize a 1-pint jar in boiling water for 5 minutes. Wash and
dry the herbs well. Chop the herbs with a knife or in a food processor. Pack the jar with the herbs and pour in the oil. Cover
with a tight-fitting lid and store in a cool, dark place. The oil
will be ready for use in 2 weeks. Strain and pour into jars or bottles. The oil will keep indefinitely in tightly covered jars or bottles at room temperature.

Biscuits

Makes about 1 dozen biscuits

A pride and joy of American cooking, biscuits are a snap to make and are wonderful with almost any meal.

Pinch salt
1 tablespoon baking powder
2 cups unbleached all-purpose flour
6 tablespoons shortening
⅔ cup milk
1 egg beaten with 1 tablespoon milk

Preheat the oven to 375°. Sift the salt, baking powder, and flour into a medium bowl. Mix in the shortening with your fingertips, a pastry cutter, or 2 knives until the mixture resembles coarse meal. Add the milk all at once and stir just until combined. Allow the dough to rest for 15 minutes, then turn out on a lightly floured board. Roll lightly to a thickness of ½ inch and cut into the desired size of rounds. Place on a greased baking sheet, brush with the egg wash, and bake in the preheated oven for 10 to 12 minutes, or until golden brown.

Muffins

Perfect as a light, low-calorie, high-fiber breakfast bread, muffins have become a morning institution. Not only are the following muffins nutritious and not too sweet, they are good showcases for winter or summer fruits, and are wonderful with homemade jams or preserves.

Winter Muffins

Makes 12 to 16 muffins

2 cups unbleached all-purpose flour
½ cup sugar
2 teaspoons baking powder
¼ teaspoon salt
1 egg
½ cup buttermilk
2 tablespoons fresh orange juice
⅓ cup vegetable oil
1 teaspoon freshly grated orange zest
1½ cups winter fruit (raisins, cranberries, sliced peeled pears or apples, or any dried fruit)
½ cup coarsely chopped pecans, walnuts, hazelnuts,* or almonds

Preheat the oven to 350°. Grease the muffin tins or spray them with nonstick spray. Sift the flour, sugar, baking powder, and salt into a large bowl. In a small bowl, beat together the egg, buttermilk, orange juice, oil, and orange zest. Stir into the flour mixture until just combined. Stir in the fruit and nuts.

Bake in the preheated oven for 20 to 25 minutes, or until golden brown. Remove from the oven and cool in the pans 5 minutes, then cool on wire racks or serve warm.

---

*If using hazelnuts, toast in a preheated 350° oven for 6 to 8 minutes, then rub off the skins in a kitchen towel or with your palms.

Summer Muffins

Makes 12 to 16 muffins

2½ cups unbleached all-purpose flour
⅓ cup sugar
2 teaspoons baking powder
¼ teaspoon salt
½ cup buttermilk
1 egg
1 teaspoon freshly grated orange zest
1½ cups fresh berries (blueberries, raspberries, currants, gooseberries, blackberries, etc.)

Preheat the oven to 350°. Reserving ½ cup of the flour, combine the dry and wet ingredients as described in the preceding recipe. Toss the berries lightly in the reserved ½ cup of flour. Stir the berries into the batter until just combined.

Bake in the preheated oven for 20 to 25 minutes, or until golden brown, cool for 5 minutes in the tins, then remove the muffins from the pans to wire racks. Let cool or serve warm.

Brioches

Makes 16 small brioches, or 1 large brioche

Brioches are wonderfully buttery and are great for breakfast with fresh preserves; they are also delicious toasted and served with salad. Use leftover brioches to make a fabulous bread pudding. The preparation time for this dough includes two slow risings, and the results are well worth it.

5 cups unbleached all-purpose flour
2 packages (4 teaspoons) active dry yeast
½ cup lukewarm (95°) milk

1 tablespoon salt
3 tablespoons sugar
2 whole eggs
8 egg yolks
1¼ cups (2½ sticks) butter, softened
1 egg beaten with 1 tablespoon milk or heavy cream

Make a sponge by placing ¾ cup of the flour in a medium bowl and making a well in the center. Mix the yeast with the milk and pour the mixture into the flour well. Stir the liquid into the flour and knead the dough into a ball. Cover the bowl and set in a warm place to rise for 30 minutes.

Place the remaining 4¼ cups flour in a large bowl and make a well in the center. Add the salt, sugar, eggs, yolks, and half of the butter. Blend together with the paddle attachment of your mixer and knead in the sponge. Add the remaining half of the butter a tablespoon at a time, mixing at medium speed and scraping the sides of the bowl every few minutes, until the butter is absorbed. Knead at medium speed for 10 to 15 minutes, or until the dough cleans the sides of the bowl. Butter a medium bowl and transfer the dough into it, cover it with plastic wrap, and refrigerate overnight.

Turn the dough out onto a lightly floured board and knead it to remove any air pockets. Roll three fourths of the dough into a ball to fit into a greased 5- or 6-cup fluted brioche mold, or make 16 balls for greased individual brioche molds or muffin cups. Form the remaining dough into 1 or 16 balls. Form a hole in the center of the larger ball or balls of dough with your finger and place the smaller ball or balls inside, sealing well. Place the dough in a warm place to rise until it almost fills the container, about 25 minutes. The dough may also be formed into a loaf and baked in a greased standard bread pan. Preheat the oven to 350°.

Brush the top of the dough with the egg wash and bake in the preheated oven for about 40 minutes for the large brioche or 10 to 15 minutes for the small brioches, or until golden brown and a cake tester inserted in the center comes out clean. Remove immediately from the pan or molds and cool on wire racks.

Note Brioche dough may be frozen just before the final rising. The final baked brioche also freezes well, wrapped tightly in a double thickness of plastic wrap.

This dough is a good foundation for many other sweet breads; your imagination is the only limit. Instead of being baked in a pan, for example, the dough may be rolled into a rectangle ½-inch thick, brushed with melted butter, and covered with any number of fruits, such as sliced apples, pears and figs; berries; or raisins or other dried fruits. Sprinkle with brown sugar and spices such as cinnamon or ginger. Roll the rectangle into a cylinder, sealing the bottom edge with egg wash, and slice. Place the slices on greased baking sheets, allow them to rise 30 minutes, brush with egg wash, and bake in a preheated 350° oven for 25 to 30 minutes.

Sourdough Bread

Makes 2 loaves

Carried by the first settlers to use as the basis for quick breads, pancakes, muffins, and Dutch-oven breads, sourdough starter was a big part of the history of the Pacific Northwest. The tang of sourdough gives a robust, earthy flavor to breads and other baked goods. There are starters still in use that have been handed down through generations.

SPONGE
1½ cups lukewarm (80°) water or milk
1½ cups Sourdough Starter, recipe following
2 cups unbleached white bread flour
1 cup whole-wheat flour

2½ cups unbleached white bread flour
1½ cups whole-wheat flour
½ cup lukewarm (80°) water

¼ cup honey or sugar
1½ teaspoons salt
Cornmeal for dusting

To make the sponge, combine the water and starter in a medium bowl and add the flours, stirring well. Cover with a towel and let sit in a warm place for 2 hours. Refrigerate the sponge overnight or up to 24 hours.

Remove the sponge from the refrigerator and place in a large bowl. Add the flours, water, honey, and salt. Knead with a dough hook on low speed until the dough forms a ball and comes away cleanly from the sides of the bowl. Continue kneading for approximately 10 minutes, or until the dough feels soft, pliable, and smooth. During this kneading, an additional ½ to ¾ cup of grains such as wheat bran, oat bran, wheat berries, barley, mixed-grain cereals, or up to ½ cup rye flour or buckwheat flour may be added. The dough may also be kneaded by hand on a lightly floured board.

Press the dough with the heels of your hands into a 6-inch round. Fold the dough onto itself, pressing down firmly with your hands. Repeat the process of folding and kneading several times during a period of 10 to 15 minutes.

Transfer the dough to a lightly oiled bowl, turn the dough to coat on all sides, cover with plastic wrap, and allow to rise for 3 hours in a warm place (85°). Punch the dough down, turn it out onto a lightly floured board, and form it into two round or long loaves.

The best method for baking bread—on a stone hearth—can be duplicated easily by placing unglazed clay tiles, a bread stone, or 8 to 10 bricks on the oven rack. In order to transfer the risen bread directly onto the heated clay or brick surface, the loaves should be placed on a wooden baker's peel or baking sheet for the final rise. Dust the peel or sheet with cornmeal and place the shaped loaves on top. Allow the dough to rise for 2 to 3 hours, or until slightly more than doubled in size. If you are not using clay tiles or bricks, the bread may rise on the same greased baking sheets on which it will bake.

Preheat the oven to 450° with the clay tiles or bricks inside.

Spray or brush the bread with water, score the top in several places with a razor blade or sharp knife, and slide the bread onto the heated surface or place it in the oven on the greased baking sheets. Bake for 10 to 12 minutes, then reduce the oven temperature to 375°. Bake for about 45 minutes longer, or until the loaves are hollow sounding when rapped on the bottom.

Note The absorption, composition, and freshness of the flours; the temperature of the dough while rising; and the degree of sourness of the starter are all varying factors in the process of bread baking. The above recipe is only a guide. The best test is the smooth, pliable *feel* of the dough during mixing and rising, so some adjustment of flour or liquid may be necessary.

SOURDOUGH STARTER
2 cups russet potatoes
3 cups boiling water
2½ to 3 cups unbleached all-purpose flour
1¼ cups cold water

Peel the potatoes, chop coarsely, and place in a 2-quart glass or ceramic container. Pour the 3 cups of boiling water over the potatoes and allow them to stand at room temperature for 12 to 18 hours, covered with a cloth. Squeeze the liquid from the potatoes and discard the potatoes. Add one cup of the flour, stir until well combined, cover the container with plastic wrap, and store in a warm place (70° to 80°) for 24 hours. Stir well and re-cover. After 24 more hours, add about 1½ cups of the flour and ½ cup of the cold water and stir well. Cover and allow to stand at room temperature for 36 to 48 hours. Finally, add the remaining flour and water. Stir well until the mixture is very sticky. Cover and set aside for 8 to 12 hours.

The starter is now ready to use. When using the starter for baking, always replace what has been withdrawn by adding an equal weight of flour and water to the starter. If 8 ounces is withdrawn, combine 1 cup flour with ½ cup water and add to the starter, stirring well.

Pasta Dough

Makes 4 servings

It's hard to resist the impulse just to cut this dough into strips, cook it al dente, and toss it with butter and herbs. Any flavorings such as herbs, tomatoes, pepper puree, etc., should be added with the eggs; the semolina should then be added gradually until the dough combines.

2⅓ cups plus 3 tablespoons semolina flour
⅓ cup unbleached all-purpose flour
8 egg yolks
1½ tablespoons olive oil
¼ teaspoon salt
1 teaspoon olive oil for tossing (optional)

In a mixing bowl fitted with a paddle attachment, combine the semolina flour, all-purpose flour, egg yolks, olive oil, and salt. Mix at medium speed, adding just enough water so that the dough is smooth and forms a ball. Or, mix the flour and mound on a work surface. Beat the yolks, oil, and salt together. Make a well in the mound of flour, pour in the yolk mixture, and mix the yolk mixture and flour together with your hands. Form into a ball and knead on a lightly floured surface for 5 to 10 minutes, or until smooth. Wrap in plastic wrap and refrigerate 1 hour.

Using a pasta machine (a hand-operated model that attaches to the work surface works best) or a rolling pin on a floured surface, roll the dough into thin sheets and cut it into fettuccine or linguine, or use the full sheets to make ravioli. Cook in a large quantity of rapidly boiling salted water until al dente; drain well. If not serving immediately, rinse with cold water and allow to drain. Toss the pasta with 1 teaspoon olive oil to prevent sticking.

Black Linguine

Makes 4 servings

3 pounds fresh squid, or 2 ounces squid ink (available in specialty food or Asian markets)
Pasta Dough, made with only 7 egg yolks

Purchase the freshest squid possible with unbroken ink sacs. Carefully remove the sacs from the tubes of the squid and save all the ink. Reserve the squid for another use, such as Squid and Octopus Salad, page 44. Boil the ink to reduce to about ¼ cup. Prepare the pasta dough, adding the squid ink and omitting 1 egg yolk.

Basil Linguine

Makes 4 servings

1¾ cups semolina flour
⅓ cup unbleached all-purpose flour
Leaves from 3 to 4 parsley sprigs
¼ cup water
¼ cup minced fresh basil
7 egg yolks

7 ½ tablespoons olive oil
¼ teaspoon salt

Combine the semolina flour and all-purpose flour in a large bowl or a food processor. Puree the parsley leaves, water, and basil in a blender until smooth. Add this liquid to the dough with the egg yolks, olive oil, and salt; blend until well combined. Or, make by hand as in the recipe for Pasta Dough, page 172.

Crab Ravioli

Makes 8 large or 18 small ravioli

Use these ravioli in Crayfish and Spot Prawn Minestrone with Dungeness Crab Ravioli, page 49, or toss them with butter and herbs for a first course or entree, or serve them with Crayfish Sauce, page 160.

Pasta Dough, page 172
3 ounces fresh cooked crab meat
½ cup whole-milk ricotta
2 eggs, beaten
1 teaspoon minced fresh chives
2 teaspoons minced fresh parsley
1 tablespoon minced fresh basil

1 teaspoon minced fresh oregano
2 garlic cloves, minced
Salt and pepper to taste
1 egg beaten with 1 tablespoon heavy cream

Prepare the pasta dough and cut it into 4 sheets 4 inches wide and 12 inches long for large ravioli, or 2 larger sheets for small ravioli. Cover the sheets with a kitchen towel while preparing the filling.

Combine the crab meat, ricotta, eggs, herbs, and garlic in a small bowl; mix well and season with salt and pepper. Lay a sheet of pasta on a lightly floured surface. Beat the egg and cream together and brush it over the entire surface of the sheet. Place 1½ tablespoons of the crab mixture in a mound on the sheet, allowing ½ inch of space around the crab mixture on all sides. Repeat to make 4 ravioli, then make another 4 ravioli on a second sheet. Or, make 18 mounds of 2 teaspoons of crab mixture on 1 large sheet of pasta to make 18 ravioli. Cover the crab with another sheet of pasta and lightly press down around each mound of crab on all sides to adhere to the bottom layer. Cut with a ravioli cutter or with a knife, crimping the edges with the tines of a fork to seal. Cover the ravioli with a towel as you prepare them.

Cook in a large quantity of slowly boiling salted water until al dente, about 10 minutes. Drain and serve immediately.

Note   If preparing in advance, drain and rinse the ravioli with cold water until cool. Carefully transfer the ravioli to a flat pan or plate lined with plastic wrap and refrigerate until ready to use.

Pie Crust

Makes 1 double-crust 9-inch pie

This is a tried and true pie crust that gives excellent results. Use it for your favorite pie filling—cherry, apple, peach, nectarine, rhubarb, pecan—the list is endless. Remember that tart, firm fruit is best for pie, and if in doubt as to the amount of sugar to use, stew a small amount of the fruit over low heat for 10 minutes. Taste and consistency will be your guides as to the sweetness and thickening necessary. A good rule of thumb is to use 1/3 cup of sugar mixed with 1 tablespoon cornstarch; toss with the fruit before spooning into the shell.

2 1/2 cups unbleached all-purpose flour
1/2 cup sugar
1/2 teaspoon salt
10 tablespoons vegetable shortening
4 tablespoons chilled unsalted butter, cut into small pieces
4 to 6 tablespoons ice water
1 egg
1 tablespoon heavy cream
1 1/2 teaspoons granulated sugar (optional)

Mix the flour, sugar, and salt together in a large bowl. Using a pastry cutter, your hands, or 2 knives, cut the shortening and butter into the flour mixture until it resembles coarse meal (or blend in a mixer with a paddle attachment). Sprinkle the water over by the tablespoon and, being careful not to overwork, mix with a spoon or your fingers only until the mixture comes together. Refrigerate for 15 to 20 minutes.

Preheat the oven to 400°. Divide the dough in half. Roll out one half on a lightly floured board, or between sheets of waxed paper, to a thickness of about 1/8 inch. Roll the dough up on the rolling pin, then roll it out over a lightly greased 9-inch pie pan. Gently press the dough into the pan, allowing it to drape over the edges. Spoon your choice of filling into the shell. Repeat the process with the remaining dough and roll it out over the filling. Trim the excess dough off the edges of the pie pan and crimp the edges together with your fingers. Whisk the egg and cream together. Brush the crust lightly with the egg wash, and sprinkle with granulated sugar if desired.

Bake in the preheated oven at 400° for the first 10 minutes, then lower the heat to 350° for 25 to 30 minutes, or until the crust is golden brown.

Tart Crust

Makes two 10-inch tart shells

2 egg yolks
1 whole egg
1 tablespoon sugar
Pinch salt
2 1/2 cups unbleached all-purpose flour
10 tablespoons unsalted butter, chilled
2 to 3 tablespoons ice water

Beat the egg yolks and whole egg together until combined. Combine the sugar, salt, and flour in a large bowl. Blend the butter in gently with your fingers, a pastry cutter, or 2 knives until the mixture resembles coarse meal. Make a well in the center and add the egg and yolks, mixing gently. Add the water by teaspoonfuls, mixing gently with a spoon or your fingers, just until the dough forms a ball.

Chill the dough for 10 minutes, then roll it out on a lightly floured board or between 2 sheets of wax paper. Line the tart shell with the pastry, trim and crimp the edges, prick the sides and bottom with a fork, then refrigerate for 20 minutes.

Preheat the oven to 375°. If the shell is to be filled after it is baked, line it with aluminum foil or parchment paper and weigh it down with dried beans, rice, or pie weights. Bake the shell in the preheated oven for 10 minutes, or until lightly browned.

Nut Crust

Follow the above recipe, using only 2 cups of flour and adding ½ cup of finely ground nuts.

Puff Pastry

Makes about 3 pounds dough

This classic puff pastry dough requires several steps and a total preparation time of about 45 minutes, most of which is to allow for the dough to rest between turns. The procedure can be easily worked into the advance preparation of a meal, and the dough will keep refrigerated for 2 to 3 days. It is preferable to divide the dough into thirds after completion. Roll one third of the dough for immediate use, then roll the remaining two thirds into ¼-inch-thick sheets about 8 by 11 inches. Wrap these sheets in plastic wrap and freeze. Allow frozen dough to thaw until it is soft enough to cut, and bake it according to the directions below.

3 cups (6 sticks) unsalted butter, chilled
3½ cups unbleached all-purpose flour
1½ cups cake flour
2 teaspoons salt
¾ cup ice water
1 egg beaten with 2 tablespoons milk

Cut ½ cup (1 stick) of the butter into small pieces. Combine both flours and the salt in a large bowl and add the cut-up ½ cup butter. With the paddle attachment of your mixer, blend on low speed until the mixture resembles coarse meal. Add the ice water and continue to blend just until the mixture combines. Form the dough into a ball, wrap it in a damp towel, and refrigerate it for 3 hours, along with the remaining 2½ cups (5 sticks) butter.

Remove the dough and the butter from the refrigerator and allow them to soften for 15 minutes. Ideally, the dough should have the same consistency as the butter. Roll the dough on a lightly floured surface into a 12-by-22-inch rectangle. Cut the butter into ⅛-inch slices and layer the dough evenly with the slices of butter, leaving a ½-inch border. Fold the border onto the butter. With the long end of the rectangle facing you, fold the left third of the dough over onto the center third. Fold the right-hand third of the dough on top of the other two. You will have a smaller rectangle with the short end facing you. Imagine this rectangle as a book with the binding on your right and the open end on your left. The open end should always be on your left at the start of each folding process.

Turn the open end of the book to face you. Roll the pastry away from you into a sheet 12 inches long. Turn the dough so that the open end of the book is on your left. Roll the pastry again until it is 30 inches in length. Mentally divide the length in half, and fold the left side of the dough to the middle, then the right side to the middle. Fold the right half over the left half, forming a new book with the binding on the right again. You have now completed 1 double turn. Cover with plastic wrap and refrigerate for 15 minutes.

Remove the dough from the refrigerator and, with the open-book end to your left, roll the dough out on a lightly floured board to a width of 30 inches. Turn the dough so that the open-book end faces you. Fold both edges into the middle and the right over the left again as described above. Repeat to make a total of 2 double turns. Cover the dough in plastic wrap and refrigerate for 15 minutes.

Repeat the process, making a total of 3 double turns. Refrigerate the dough again and make the fourth and final double turn.

Cover the dough tightly in plastic wrap and store in the refrigerator. To bake, preheat the oven to 450°. Roll the dough out to a thickness of ¼ inch and cut it into any desired shape. After rolling and cutting, place the dough on slightly moistened baking sheets and refrigerate it until firm. Brush with the egg wash and bake in the preheated oven for 10 minutes, or until it is puffed and lightly browned, then lower the heat to 300° and bake the pastry 15 to 20 minutes longer, or until crisp.

Basic Buttercream

Makes about 3½ cups

2 cups (4 sticks) unsalted butter, softened
8 egg yolks
¾ cup sugar

Whip the butter with an electric mixer, first on low, then on high, until light and creamy. Whisk the yolks and the sugar well in a heatproof bowl. Immerse the bowl in a pan of boiling water and whip constantly until the eggs are very thick and hot, about 10 minutes. Transfer to another bowl, set it in ice, and refrigerate, whisking occasionally, until completely cold. Slowly whip the chilled egg yolk mixture into the creamed butter until the buttercream is light and fluffy.

Pastry Cream

Makes 2½ cups

This is a simple recipe that yields perfect results. It is preferable to use only a minimal amount of sugar, as many of the desserts that call for pastry cream are quite sweet. Try whisking honey into the cream when it is thoroughly chilled if you wish, as a substitute for the sugar.

6 egg yolks
4 whole eggs
1⅔ cups heavy cream

2 tablespoons to ¼ cup sugar, or 1 tablespoon honey
½ vanilla bean, split lengthwise
1 teaspoon cornstarch mixed with 1 teaspoon water
1 teaspoon Grand Marnier, rum, kirsch, or bourbon

In a medium bowl, whisk together the yolks and eggs. Combine the cream, sugar, and vanilla bean in a medium saucepan and bring to a simmer over medium heat. Whisk ½ cup of the hot cream into the eggs in a thin stream to temper them. Whisk the tempered eggs into the hot cream mixture and, whisking constantly, lower the heat and cook until the custard begins to thicken (about 1 minute). Whisk the cornstarch into the cream by drops and, just before the cream bubbles, strain it through a fine sieve into a medium bowl. Whisk thoroughly.

The cream may now cool to room temperature, or it can be set in a bowl of ice if desired. When thoroughly cool, refrigerate until the cream is set. Remove the vanilla bean. Flavor the cream with liqueur after it is thoroughly chilled.

Custard

Makes 2 cups

Follow the above recipe for Pastry Cream, decreasing the egg yolks to 4 and the whole eggs to 2, and omitting the cornstarch.

Fresh Fruit Napoleons

Serves 4

One of the best ways to showcase fresh fruits is in Napoleons: layers of puff pastry, pastry cream, and fruit.

Pastry Cream, page 177
Dough for Puff Pastry, page 175
2 cups sliced fresh fruit (peaches, nectarines, pears, pitted
  cherries, oranges, tangerines, etc.) or berries
Powdered sugar for dusting
Caramel Sauce, page 31

Prepare the pastry cream and refrigerate until chilled. Prepare the puff pastry dough. Preheat the oven to 400°. Cut the sheets of pastry into 4 strips about 4 inches wide and 10 inches long. Place the strips on a baking sheet sprinkled with water and prick them all over with a fork. Top the sheets with a cake cooling rack to compress the sheets slightly during baking. Bake in the preheated oven for 10 minutes, then lower the heat to 250° and bake the pastry for another 15 to 20 minutes, or until light brown and crisp. Cool on wire racks.

Press the puff pastry sheets lightly with the palm of your hand. Cut each strip into 3 equal pieces. Spread 2 to 3 tablespoons of pastry cream on 1 layer. Top this with fresh fruit. Spread another puff pastry piece with a layer of cream and place that on top of the fruit. Repeat the procedure with the final layer. Smooth the sides with pastry cream. To serve, dust with powdered sugar and serve with warm caramel sauce.

Candied Ginger

Makes ½ cup

¼ cup julienne-cut peeled fresh ginger root
½ cup water
5 tablespoons sugar
1 tablespoon distilled white wine vinegar

Place the ginger in a small saucepan, add cold water to cover, and bring to a boil; drain. Add the ½ cup water, sugar, and vinegar, and bring to a simmer over very low heat. Continue to simmer until the ginger is tender and the syrup is clear and shiny, about 20 minutes. Keep warm if to be used within 1 or 2 hours, or pour into a covered container and store at room temperature. Candied ginger will keep indefinitely.

Basic Custard Ice Cream

Makes 1 quart ice cream

This ice cream is the basis for an array of ice creams that can be prepared by adding fresh fruits, flavorings, nuts, or liqueurs. It is velvety, rich, easy to prepare, and unsurpassed for flavor and creaminess.

2½ cups heavy cream
½ cup half and half
½ cup sugar
½ vanilla bean, split lengthwise
12 egg yolks

In a heavy, medium saucepan, combine the cream, half and half, sugar, and vanilla bean and warm over low heat to 160° on a candy thermometer; do not boil.

While the cream is warming, beat the egg yolks on medium speed with an electric mixer for 5 to 8 minutes, or until the yolks begin to thicken slightly. When the cream reaches 160°, pour ½ cup of the hot mixture into the yolks, beating constantly. When combined, beat in the remaining cream in a steady stream, and continue to beat the custard on medium speed for 5 minutes.

Allow the custard to sit in the bowl at room temperature, stirring frequently, until cooled. If you wish to prepare the ice cream immediately, immerse the bowl in a larger bowl filled with ice. The custard may be refrigerated overnight if desired. Follow the manufacturer's instructions for the ice cream maker to freeze the ice cream.

CHOCOLATE ICE CREAM

Add 6 to 8 ounces melted bittersweet chocolate to the still-warm custard. Cool and freeze.

COFFEE ICE CREAM

Combine ½ cup very strong coffee, 1 ounce melted semisweet chocolate, and 2 tablespoons instant coffee powder. Add to the warm custard, cool, and freeze.

HONEY ICE CREAM

Add ⅓ cup honey to the cream while heating; omit the sugar. Cool and freeze.

PRALINE ICE CREAM

Combine 1¼ cups sugar and ¼ cup water and cook to 248° on a candy thermometer. Add 1⅔ cups toasted nuts and pour the mixture onto a greased baking sheet or marble slab. Cool, break into bite-sized pieces, and add to the partially frozen ice cream.

STRAWBERRY ICE CREAM

Puree 2 pints strawberries with ½ cup sugar. Add to the cooled custard. When the ice cream is partially frozen, add 1½ pints halved or quartered fresh strawberries.

RASPBERRY ICE CREAM

Puree 2 pints fresh raspberries with ⅓ cup sugar. Add to the cooled custard and freeze. If you like, you can also add 1 cup of whole raspberries to the ice cream when it is partially frozen.

PEACH OR NECTARINE ICE CREAM

Puree 4 peeled peaches or nectarines and the juice of 1 orange with ½ cup sugar. Add the puree to the cooled custard and freeze. Add 3 cut-up peaches or nectarines to the ice cream when it is almost frozen.

PLUM ICE CREAM

Pit 8 to 10 plums (Mirabelle, Damson, Friar, greengage, Italian) and quarter if large. Freeze the custard according to directions and add the plums when it is partially frozen.

Basic Syrup for Sorbets

Makes about 1 quart

Sorbets are the quintessence of ripe, flavorful fruit and are the perfect dessert in any season. They are also fantastic layered in a terrine with fresh fruits, sliced, and served with a fresh fruit sauce.

4½ cups water
5½ cups sugar

Place the water and sugar in a medium saucepan over high heat and stir until the sugar is dissolved. Bring the syrup to a full boil. Immediately remove from the heat and pour into a large heatproof bowl or canning jar. Cool completely before use. This syrup will keep for months refrigerated. Following is a sampler of possibilities.

APRICOT

Simmer 5 cups apricots in 1⅔ cups syrup for 5 minutes. Puree, cool, and freeze.

RED OR BLACK CURRANT

Puree 3 quarts ripe currants and mix the puree (about 2½ cups) with 1⅔ cups syrup; freeze.

LEMON

Mix 1 cup fresh lemon juice, ¾ cup water and 1⅓ cups syrup; freeze.

RASPBERRY

Mix 3 cups uncooked pureed raspberries with 2 cups syrup; freeze.

STRAWBERRY

Mix 2½ cups uncooked pureed strawberries with 2 cups syrup; freeze.

MANGO

Mix 2 cups uncooked mango puree, 1⅓ cups syrup, and the juice of 1 lime; freeze.

MELON

Mix 2½ cups melon puree (from 2 pounds of melon) with 1⅔ cups syrup; freeze.

GRAPEFRUIT

Mix 3 cups grapefruit juice with 1½ cups syrup; freeze.

PEACH

Mix 3½ cups peach puree (from 1¾ pounds peaches) and 1⅔ cups syrup; freeze.

CIDER

Mix 3½ cups cider with 2 cups syrup; freeze.

PEAR

Mix 3 cups pureed very ripe pears with 1½ cups syrup; freeze.

Following is a list of merchants, dealers, growers, and other sources who are the soup-to-nuts providers of the foods of the Pacific Northwest. Their effort and love for their work are major reasons why these foods have reached a pinnacle of quality. Unfortunately, we cannot possibly list all of the many hundreds of suppliers in the Northwest. Contacts are listed as a source of additional information and suppliers.

Seafood

University Seafood, 1317 N.E. 47th Street, Seattle, WA 98105, (206) 632–3900/3700. The finest-quality seafood, smoked fish and poultry, fresh poultry and game, shipped anywhere overnight. All major credit cards accepted.

Fishworks! Jon Rowley, Fisherman's Terminal, Bldg. C-10, Seattle, WA 98119, (206) 283–7566. A resource for all fisheries information.

Meats

K and N Meats, 2900 Fourth Avenue South, Seattle, WA 98134, (206) 628–4811. A full line of Northwest beef, veal, lamb, pork, and poultry, shipped anywhere overnight. All major credit cards accepted.

Sausages

Bavarian Meats, 2934 Western Avenue, Seattle, WA 98115, (206) 448–3540. A full line of high-quality sausages, shipped anywhere overnight. All major credit cards accepted.

Dry Goods, Oils, and Vinegars

Borrochini Distributing, 1962 First Avenue South, Seattle, WA 98134, (206) 682–1590.

DeLaurenti Foods, Pike Place Market, Seattle, WA 98115, (206) 622–0141.

Chocolates and Candies

Fran's, 2805 East Madison Avenue, Seattle, WA 98115, (206) 322–6511. They will ship anywhere overnight. All major credit cards accepted.

Coffee, Tea, and Specialty Candies

Starbucks Coffee, 2010 Airport Way South, Seattle, WA 98135, (206) 447–1575. They will ship anywhere in North America overnight. All major credit cards accepted.

Oriental Foods

Uwajimaya, 519 Sixth Avenue South, Seattle, WA 98104, (206) 624–6248. A complete line of Asian foods, produce, meats, fish, and cookware, shipped anywhere overnight. All major credit cards accepted.

Cheeses

Quillasacut Cheese, Rich and Laura Lea Misterly, 2409 Pleasant Valley Road, Rice, WA 99167, (509) 738–2011. Several varieties of soft-ripened and hard cheeses. They will ship anywhere in North America.

Rogue River Valley Creamery, P.O. Box 3606, Central Point, OR 97502, (503) 664–2233. Oregon blue cheese.

Washington State University Creamery, Troy Hall, Rm. 101, Pullman, WA 99164, (509) 335–7516. Cougar Gold Cheddar.

Herbs, Vegetables, and Fruits

Orchard Street, Mary Schultz, 143 Charles Street, Monroe, WA 98272, (206) 794–6157. Certified organic fruits, vegetables, and herbs; antique apples and espaliered apple trees; specialty and rare lettuces. They will ship anywhere. C.O.D. and charge accounts are available.

Silver Bay Herb Farm, Mary Preuss, 9511 Tracyton Boulevard, Bremerton, WA 98310, (206) 692–1340. Specialty herbs and vegetables and sea beans shipped anywhere overnight. C.O.D. and charge accounts are available.

Country Store and Farm, Cindy Olsen and Beth Killner, Route 2, P.O. Box 304, Vashon Island, WA 98070, (206) 322–3072. Certified organic herbs, seasonal salads, vinegars, edible flowers, and filberts shipped anywhere. C.O.D. and charge accounts are available.

Martins Farm, P.O. Box 1521, Puyallup, WA 98371, (206) 922–3324/6126. Certified organic vegetables and herbs shipped anywhere. C.O.D. and charge accounts are available.

Pike Place Market, Mariann Solseng, 85 Pike Street, Rm. 500, Seattle, WA 98121, (206) 682–7453. A contact source for farmers, growers, and suppliers.

Walla Walla Growers Association, 210 North 11th Street, Walla Walla, WA 99362, (509) 529–3253. Walla Walla sweet onions shipped anywhere overnight. All major credit cards are accepted.

Island Meadow Farm, Bob and Bonnie Origson, Vashon Island, WA 98070, (206) 463–9065. Hazelnuts, walnuts, and chestnuts.

Puget Sound Mycological Society, Center for Urban Horticulture, University of Washington, Seattle, WA 98195, (206) 522–6031. A contact source for all varieties of wild mushrooms in the Pacific Northwest.

Bickford Orchards, Monte and Penny Bickford, 3300 N.W. Empire Street, East Wenatchee, WA 98802, (509) 884–8840. Cherries, apples, and peaches.

INDEX